jewels
of PERSIA
exotic dishes from the ancient land

ISBN: 978-0-9954079-0-9 (hardbound)
ISBN: 978-0-9954079-1-6 (e-book)

Published by: Sharon B-Nejad 2016
Text and photographs copyright © Sharon B-Nejad 2016

Design, photography and styling: Sharon B-Nejad
Print and bound by: ingramspark.com

Jewels of Persia: Perth, Western Australia
jewelsofpersia.com.au

about the jewels

This book symbolises a period in my life, which has been rich in personal growth, fun times and, finally, enlightenment.

Fifteen years ago, in its humble beginnings, *Jewels of Persia* was nothing more than a simple collection of Persian recipes. As a young newly-wed, I started to try out and collect these recipes, in an attempt to make my husband a happy chap.

At the time, I couldn't find a single Persian cookbook in the bookshops. So, as a former graphic designer, I set out on a mission to make a small home-made book for personal use. Subsequently, it occurred to me that photos would help with the visualisation process. The first digital camera I owned took two AA batteries that would last about 12 minutes. That made things challenging and the quality was poor, but things progressed.

My husband always candidly told me if the dishes and photos were not quite as they should be, and suggested ways to improve them. And so I persisted, made changes, and more changes until the recipes and photos finally evolved into what they are today. My overall goal was to recreate these recipes as close to the traditional ones as possible.

As time passed, the recipes evolved and my love of cooking and photography grew even further. And then one day my husband stopped me and said that I had spent enough time on this project and should get it printed.

The name *Jewels of Persia* came about because of the many beautiful ingredients resembling jewels used in Persian cooking, such as pomegranates and barberries. So finally, here it is. I hope you enjoy it and have as much fun with it as I have.

jewels of PERSIA

exotic dishes from the ancient land

WRITTEN & PHOTOGRAPHED BY

sharon b-nejad

www.jewelsofpersia.com.au

لطفاً با ظرف شیشه ای با آب... شیشه

Manoucheri House, Kashan

Once a historical private residence, Manoucheri House is now beautifully restored as a boutique hotel. Situated in the heart of Kashan's historic neighborhood, it boasts eight private guest rooms. Each has unique architectural details and faces onto a peaceful courtyard with a reflecting pool and gardens bearing local fruit.

contents

❧⸻⸺⸻❧

What is Persian cuisine?

Most people expect Persian cuisine to be hot to the taste and heavily loaded with spices. However, this is quite far from the truth. Persian cuisine is perfumed, rich and elegant, but generally not hot and spicy.

It is rich in fruits, vegetables, meats, legumes and nuts of all kinds. These easily obtainable ingredients are paired with the freshest of abundantly grown herbs and delicate spice combinations such as saffron, turmeric, cinnamon, cardamom and dried limes. In doing this, they have achieved a well-balanced, flavoursome diet, full of health benefits.

Persians have always been avid believers in the powerful healing effects of certain ingredients and this is certainly reflected in their food combinations, even today. Only now are we in the Western world embracing the knowledge that Persian people have understood and developed over millennia, such as the benefits of pomegranates, okra, turmeric, cinnamon, yoghurt, nuts and so on.

The Persian housewife will only purchase ingredients that are in season, when they are freshest, most abundant and offer the best value for money. She will then cleverly use these ingredients to make pickles, jams and purées; she will even cook and freeze herbs to add to stews months later.

Persians enjoy a distinct, sour taste, sometimes mixed with a little sweetness. The addition of dried limes, pomegranates, verjuice, unripened plums and barberries is commonplace in Persian cuisine. Numerous recipes contained in this book are testament to this delicious combination that I hope you will discover and enjoy.

Most Persian dishes are often quite labour-intensive, as they are cooked slowly, simmering gently over extended periods of time. All this effort does, in turn, achieve deliciously tender, melt-in-your-mouth meats, which perfectly complement the vegetables and spices.

Traditionally, the techniques and skills for cooking Persian food have been passed down from one generation to the next. Therefore, there has been no need for written recipes and cookbooks are almost unheard of.

It was commonplace that each family member had a role in helping prepare the food: one cleaned, another chopped vegetables and herbs or went to buy meat or fresh bread at the market. With the onset of modernisation, this way of life has naturally changed over the recent years.

Essential accompaniments

Four essential accompaniments are served alongside almost every Persian meal. The first is an abundance of different fresh herbs such as basil, coriander, mint, parsley and tarragon. These are said to aid digestion and freshen the breath. The second is the indispensable fresh flatbread such as lavash, taftoon or barbari that are deemed a staple food in their own right. Third are a selection of pickled vegetables and relishes and fourth a bowl of thick, natural yoghurt.

Meat

In Persian cuisine, lamb, veal and poultry are top on the shopping list. Fish and some seafood are popular throughout the southern and Caspian Sea regions, but purely because of geography have lacked favour in the cities tucked away from the coastal areas. As in any other Muslim country, pork consumption is forbidden for the general population. However, cleverly enough, they have managed to manufacture processed meats with an astonishing resemblance to ham, but made from other types of meat.

Kebabs

Kebabs are an integral part of Persian cuisine. They are usually marinated in a combination of minced onion, lime juice, saffron, spices and sometimes yoghurt. They are often consumed in restaurants, and traditionally not cooked at home by the housewife due to the specialised skills needed in the preparation of the meat as well as the cooking. However, the recipes that follow are the culmination of numerous trials to get the best results possible at home.

continued...

Persian rice

Rice, of course, is a staple, and Persian rice dishes are like no other. Aged Basmati is best for creating the beautiful rice dishes in the recipes that follow. The preparation of rice is rather elaborate, often taking a couple of hours. This process usually involves rinsing, soaking, boiling, straining and, finally, steaming. This method creates wonderful, fluffy rice, with less starch, in which each grain elongates and doesn't stick to the next.

The parboiled rice is also often mixed with combinations of meat, poultry, dried fruits, berries, nuts, herbs and yoghurt and then steamed. These combinations produce dishes that are delicious, colourful and very fragrant.

Persian rice is uniquely famous for its golden crust known as the Tah Dig, which can be made from thin slices of potato, flatbread or the rice itself (see page 131).

All sweet things

After the meal, fresh fruit is usually consumed rather than a baked pudding or cake. Persians, however, love cookies, pastries, sugar cubes or fresh dates with their tea anytime of the day or night. The cookies are often made from a variety of different types of flour and nuts, usually with the addition of cardamom and rose water.

Iran is famous for Gaz, which is a kind of nougat usually with pistachio, Sohan, a delicious saffron brittle and Pashmak, a chewy cotton candy. The Persian housewife does not usually make these items at home, due to the level of difficulty in their preparation, and also because they are readily available in shops.

the people

Persian hospitality

Persians are renowned worldwide for their generous, hospitable natures. Persians believe a guest is a gift from heaven and always make sure they prepare a little extra, just on the off chance a visitor should drop by unannounced.

Like most, I had some preconceived ideas as to what I thought Iran and its people would be like. Despite what I saw in our news and media, Iranians love foreigners. I dare say even more than their fellow country people and go well out of their way to make them feel welcomed and content, regardless of their personal comfort or situation.

After five visits to Iran, I am still humbled and amazed by the hospitality and kindness I have witnessed from friends, family and strangers alike. Many young women and even a few men have stopped me on the busy streets, merely to make conversation, take a photo or practise their English, which is usually quite good. They always ask if I am enjoying my travels, and if I like the food and historical sites.

Each time we visit Iran we have stayed with friends and family, sometimes for up to six weeks. During that entire period, they are happy to give up their bedroom, sleep on the floor, drive us wherever we want to go, cook the most delicious meals every day, and still look happy.

What about the dress code?

People often think every woman in Iran must cover themselves from head to toe in a black cloak. While this is true in some cases, especially older women or women holding government positions, the young women, especially on the streets of Tehran, have a very different approach to dressing within the bounds of these restrictions. It is commonplace to see women wearing the most fashionable, tightest, shortest outfits possible, ridiculously high-heeled shoes and just a wisp of a scarf to cover their hair. What about make-up and hair? Let's just say less might be better, but I guess they are just rebelling in their way and I say good luck to them.

The nation

For a nation of over 75 million, they seem to coexist quite harmoniously. All queues are round; no straight lines here. They drive everywhere at mind-blowing speeds, with little regard for rules, lanes or even red lights, making crossing the road a very hairy challenge. However, I have witnessed minimal road rage and seen motorists prepared to stop at any second for a pedestrian or other motorist.

The historically significant sites in Iran are ancient treasures indeed. It is, however, a shame that, despite the enormity of the UNESCO World Heritage sites, disproportionately little has been done to promote tourism or even preserve them for posterity. But this is slowly changing.

To sum up, I hope this book gives you a taste of the real Iran, its people and their wonderful cuisine.

traditional restaurant

Esfahan, the former capital of Iran has one of the largest city squares in the world. It is called Naqsh-e Jahan Square and is a UNESCO World Heritage site. This restaurant, bearing the same name, is a great example of a traditional-style Persian restaurant. Complete with day beds, it is customary to remove your shoes and sit cross-legged while eating your food.

barberries

Grown predominantly in the eastern region of Khorasan, barberries come from the dried fruit of the barberry bush. They have a delicious, sour taste, creating the perfect complement to chicken dishes.

dried rose petals

These wonderfully fragrant petals can be added to tea, yoghurt and rice dishes. They also come in a ground form, in two of the Spice Blends, found on page 20.

dried limes

Dried limes impart a sour, tart taste to dishes. They can be left in the food and eaten, or be removed prior to serving. Dried limes feature in Ghormeh Sabzi, a delicious, herbed lamb stew found on page 104.

sumac

Sumac is a coarse spice that is sour in taste. It is predominantly served with kebabs, but can also be added to salads. It comes from a wild berry which grows throughout the Middle East.

tamarind

Tamarind is a fruit that grows as a pod. It is sweet and sour in taste and high in vitamin B as well as calcium. It features in the dish Ghalieh Mahi, a fantastic coriander and fish stew found on page 109.

kashk

Kashk is a thick, creamy produce, similar to whey. It has a distinctly sour taste, similar to aged yoghurt. It is sold as a ready-made liquid and also in dried form. As it is somewhat difficult to find and has quite a strong taste, you may wish to substitute it with sour cream or yoghurt.

pomegranate purée

Pomegranate purée is processed from the juice of a sour variety of pomegranate. It gives dishes a beautiful, rich colouring and flavour when added. Famous for its pairing with crushed walnuts, it is found in this combination in Fesenjoon, a delicious chicken stew, found on page 111.

musir

Musir is a wild Persian garlic that can often be found in dried form. It must be soaked in hot water to soften, prior to use. It is often found in pickle recipes, but also features in Mast Musir, a yoghurt dish that usually accompanies kebabs. It can be found on page 45.

pantry staples

basmati rice

Famous for its grain length, fragrance and delicate flavour, aged basmati rice stays firm and separates during cooking, making it perfect for Persian rice dishes.

reshteh

Reshteh are thin, round noodles made from wheat. Symbolic of the unravelling of life's problems, they feature during Persian New Year celebrations. Angel hair pasta, capellini and linguini are all suitable substitutes.

black-eyed beans

Black-eyed beans are small, white legumes with a prominent black spot. Black-eyed beans are frequently used in Persian soups and stews.

green lentils

Green lentils frequently feature in numerous Persian soup dishes. They are also sprouted as a part of the Persian New Year celebrations.

barley

Barley is a whole grain, high in protein and fibre. It is a prominent ingredient in many Persian soup dishes.

yellow split peas

Yellow split peas are a type of legume which split naturally once dried, hence their name. They are one of the essential ingredients in Gheimeh, a lamb and split pea stew found on page 115.

red kidney beans

Red kidney beans get their name from their uncanny resemblance, both in shape and colour, to miniature kidneys. They are found in many Persian soups and stews.

white beans

Dried white beans are cooked by boiling for several hours. Hence they are commonly presoaked. This shortens cooking times and results in more evenly cooked beans.

dried fruits

Persians have a love affair with dried fruits and use them, very cleverly, in a variety of dishes. You will often find them in Persian soups, stews, rice dishes and sweets. They often have a sweet and sour taste, which Persians adore. The above photo is of a small food bazaar, selling all types of dried fruits, nuts, spices and staples in the north of Iran.

liquid saffron

1 tsp saffron threads
pinch of salt or sugar
250 ml boiling water

1   In a mortar and pestle, pound the saffron threads with the salt or sugar, until a fine powder is formed. The addition of the salt or sugar makes it easier to grind the saffron.

2   Place the ground saffron in a small jar and add the boiling water. Stir to release the colour and allow to infuse and cool for 30 minutes.

3   Once completely cooled, seal and store in the refrigerator until needed.

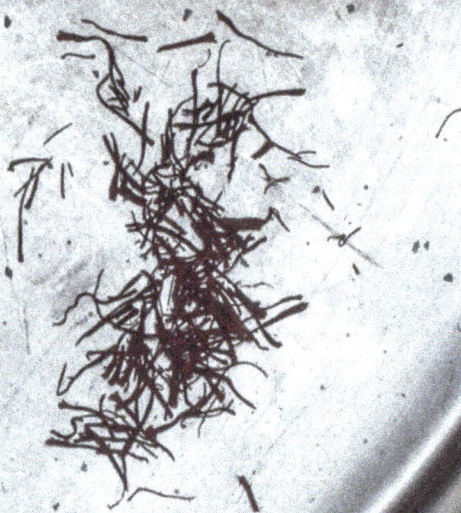

fact

Only three individual stigmas are formed by each saffron crocus flower. Each stigma, when dried, turns into a single strand of saffron. Saffron must be individually handpicked due to its delicate nature. This makes it an extremely labour-intensive process and is why saffron is so expensive.

pistachios

Pistachios feature in many Persian dishes, both sweet and savoury. They can be used whole, slivered and crushed. Persians love to eat them in season, fresh and unroasted.

walnuts

Walnuts are an excellent source of vitamin E and actively raise good cholesterol levels. In Persian cuisine, walnuts are often paired with pomegranates and sour grape juice.

fetta cheese

Fetta is common at the Persian breakfast table. It is often eaten with warm Barbari bread, slices of tomato and cucumber.

fresh herbs

Fresh herbs such as mint, coriander, parsley and basil are commonly eaten alongside a main meal to aid digestion and freshen the breath. Fresh herbs are also used in many Persian dishes from soups, to stews and egg dishes.

dill

Dill can be used fresh or in its dried form. It is a known appetiser, aids in digestive health and is also known to reduce inflammation. It features in many Persian dishes, including rice dishes, soups, yoghurt and meatballs.

pomegranate

Persians are huge fans of the pomegranate. Known as a superfood, they are cherished for their beauty and distinct sour taste. It is commonplace in Iran to see vendors selling pomegranate juice by the glassful. A thick, dark-coloured purée is also used in many dishes.

eggplant

Eggplants are known for their deep shiny, deep-purple skin as well as their unique, mildly bitter taste. They are available in varying shapes and sizes, from long and thin, to the large, oval, common variety. They are often cooked over coals, imparting a delicious smoky flavour to dishes.

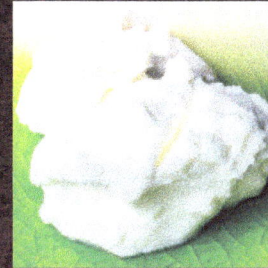

yoghurt

Greek-style yoghurt is high in calcium, probiotics, vitamin B12, protein and iodine. It is served alongside almost every Persian meal except fish. When combined with rice and chicken, or rice, lamb and spinach, it makes a delicious dish called Tah Chin, which can be found on pages 133 and 157 respectively.

advieh
SPICE BLENDS

advieh khorosht

SPICE BLEND FOR STEWS

4 tbsp dried rose petals, crushed
4 tbsp ground cinnamon
4 tbsp ground cardamom
1 tsp black pepper
2 tsp ground nutmeg
2 tbsp ground cumin
1 tsp ground coriander
2 tsp dried lime powder

advieh polo

SPICE BLEND FOR RICE DISHES

4 tbsp dried rose petals, crushed
4 tbsp ground cinnamon
4 tbsp ground cardamom
2 tbsp ground cumin

advieh torshi

SPICE BLEND FOR PICKLES

2 tbsp ground cinnamon
1 tbsp ground cardamom
3 tbsp ground ginger
4 tbsp cumin seeds
1 tsp peppercorns
1 tsp ground star anise
1 tsp turmeric
3 tbsp ground coriander

For all blends, mix the spices together, seal and store in an airtight container in a dark place.

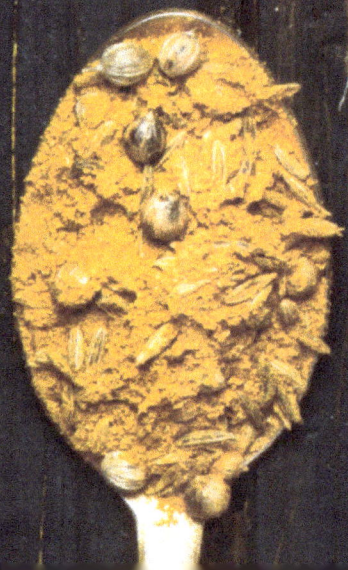

everyday spices

saffron

Saffron is used widely throughout Persian cuisine. It is used to give colour as well as flavour, to sweet and savoury dishes. It is the most expensive spice in the world, due to its labour-intensive picking process. Persian saffron is known to be the best in the world due to its rich colour and strong flavour.

turmeric

In Persian cuisine, turmeric is the second most frequently used spice. It provides a vibrant colour and an earthy, mustard flavour. Persians have known about its health benefits for thousands of years. It is also sometimes used as a cheaper substitute for saffron.

cinnamon

Cinnamon is another key spice in Persian cuisine and features in numerous sweet as well as savoury dishes. Cinnamon bark is also used to make a deliciously refreshing, flavoursome tea, found on page 234.

fenugreek seeds

Fenugreek seeds have a slightly bitter, curry-like flavour. They are hard, oval seeds about 3 mm in length. Fenugreek seeds feature in Ghalieh Mahi, a fantastic coriander and fish stew, found on page 109.

cardamom

Cardamom pods come from a plant belonging to the ginger family. It is a warm, earthy spice, sweet in flavour, almost like eucalyptus. It is frequently used in its ground form in numerous stews and desserts. The pods also feature in a delicious Persian tea, found on page 234.

dried lime powder

Dried lime powder is a powder made from the dried, crushed black Persian limes. It has a tangy, citrus taste and is added to many Persian stews. As it is difficult to source, you can grind your own, using whole dried, black limes.

advieh

Advieh is a blend of spices used in stews, rice dishes and pickles. The blend varies for each purpose, but common spices are cinnamon, cardamom and cumin. The three spice blends can be found on page 20.

nutmeg

Nutmeg has a warm, sweet, spicy flavour. It is commonly used in its powdered form but can also be used grated, fresh from the pod. It features in many Persian soups and stews.

cherries

Cherries are very popular in Iran and come in three varieties: pink, black and sour. The sour cherry is the most popular and is often made into jams and syrups. It also features in Albaloo polo, a delicious lamb and rice dish.
Spring time in Iran is a must to see the beautiful cherry blossoms.

utensils

metal skewers

Persian kebab skewers come in three widths. The first is 0.5 cm wide and is for tomatoes. The second is 1 cm wide and is for grilling chicken and meat. The third is 2 cm wide and is for cooking Koobideh, a kebab made from lamb mince, found on page 165.

rice serving spoons

A rice serving spoon is traditionally a large, flat, stainless steel spoon. It is the perfect shape and size for transferring Persian rice from the serving tray to your plate.

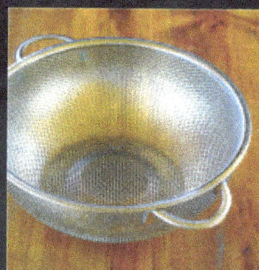

colander

A colander is essentially a bowl-shaped utensil, with holes. It is used for straining rice, pasta and vegetables and is also known as a sieve. It is important when buying a colander for rice, that the holes are smaller than a grain of rice.

earthenware pots

Heat is absorbed slowly and evenly throughout earthenware pots. They also have high heat retention, making them great for slow cooking in the oven. Ab goosht, a comforting, slow-cooked, lamb and chickpea stew is traditionally cooked in this type of pot. The recipe can be found on page 71.

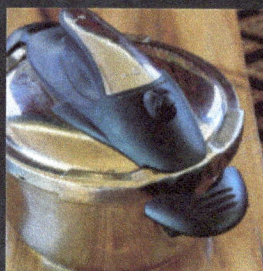

pressure cooker

Though not essential, the pressure cooker is a time-saving device well suited to Persian cooking. Cubed lamb can cook in as little as 15 minutes, opposed to 2 hours in a traditional pan. It is also well suited for cooking dried beans and pulses rapidly.

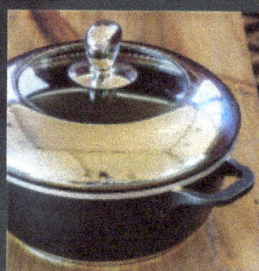

heavy-based pans

These pans are best suited for creating Persian rice dishes. The bottom of the pan is made from a thick metal, which conducts the heat evenly as well as retains it. It is essential in creating the perfect Tah Dig, which is the crispy bottomed rice, found on page 131.

serving spoons

These types of spoons are perfect for serving Persian stews. Their design holds an ample amount of the sauce, as well as some of the meat or vegetables.

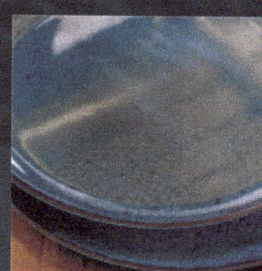

rice trays

Persian rice, unlike Asian, is not served in bowls. It is usually spooned onto round or oval, flat trays and piled up to form a mound. A round tray is essential for a dish where the rice is flipped to serve, rather than spooned out. An example of this is Tah Chin, a delicious saffron rice, with yoghurt and chicken, found on page 133.

Copper Bazaar, Esfahan

The Esfahan Bazaar is the longest covered market in the world and is also one of the oldest, dating back to the 17th century. As you enter the copper bazaar, the sounds of tapping and hammering fill the air; the process is mesmerising to watch. Hand-beaten trays, platters, pots, pans and utensils all beckon you for a closer look. The workmanship is amazing.

flatbreads

Fresh flatbread is a vital accompaniment to most meals in the Persian household. It is often served alongside rice, herbs and cheese, soups and eggplant dishes.

taftoon

Taftoon is a thin, crusty flatbread with a spongy texture. It is usually oval or round in shape with characteristic holes throughout. It is a yeast-leavened bread made with wholemeal and white flours. It comes with nigella or sesame seeds but is also sold plain. Taftoon often accompanies kebabs.

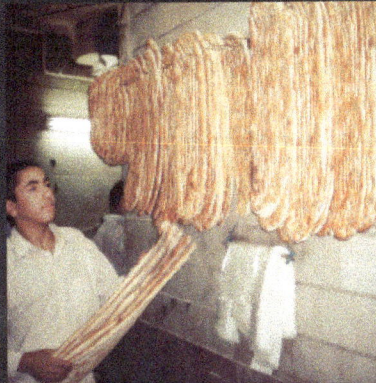

barbari

Barbari is long and oval in shape and thicker than other Persian flatbreads. It is a yeast-leavened bread made with white flour. Although it is fluffy and light in texture, it has a crispy bottom. Traditionally baked in a wood-fired oven, it comes with a delicate charcoal flavour. Barbari is popular at the Persian breakfast table and is often served alongside cheeses, cream, jams and honey. It may also be served with soups and dips.

lavash

Lavash is the thinnest of the flatbreads. The dough is rolled out, placed on a baker's cushion and slapped against the hot walls of a clay oven. Lavash is soft when fresh, but dries out quickly and becomes brittle. It is used to wrap kebabs and sandwiches when fresh, and when dried, is broken and put in soups.

sangak

Sangak is a wholemeal flatbread, usually triangular in shape. It has a slightly sour flavour and spongy texture. Unlike other flatbreads, it is baked on a bed of stones. This method of baking on the stony surface is what gives Sangak its uneven thickness, including some small holes. It often comes with sesame or poppy seeds on top, but is also sold plain.

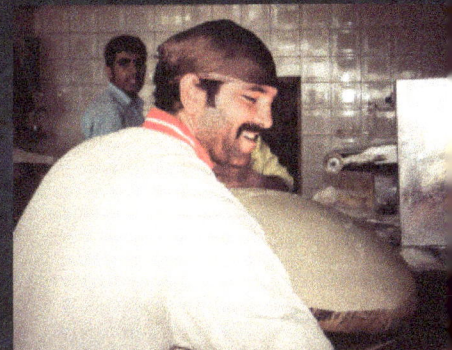

Top photo:
Baker making taftoon in a traditional tanoor oven.

Bottom photo:
Queuing for fresh bread in downtown Tehran.

dolmeh

Dolmeh is a dish in which seasonal vegetables and fruits are hollowed out and stuffed with fillings of rice, meat, legumes and herbs.

It is a popular dish in Iran, with the most delicious made from young grapevine leaves. Tomatoes, eggplants, zucchini, quince, cabbage leaves and capsicums can also be used.

appetisers & sides

30 mast khiar
cucumber, dill & yoghurt dip with
dried rose petals

33 jewelled salad
pomegranate, mint & cucumber salad

34 sabzi mahkloot
fresh herb platter with walnuts & fetta

37 borani bademjoon
smoky eggplant, garlic & yoghurt dip

38 zeytoon parvardeh
olives marinated in pomegranate, walnut & mint

42 borani esfanaj
spiced spinach & yoghurt dip

baked garlic 44

mast musir 45
yoghurt with wild Persian garlic

salad olivieh 46
Persian chicken & potato salad

mirza ghassemi 49
smoky eggplant with garlic, tomato & egg

salad shirazi 51
Shiraz cucumber & tomato salad

kahoo va sekanjebin 52
mini cos lettuce with vinegar syrup

dolmeh barg 55
stuffed vine leaves

[pronounced / most khee-yar]

mast khiar

CUCUMBER, DILL & YOGHURT DIP WITH DRIED ROSE PETALS

serves 6 | **prep** 10m | **cook** nil

1 small Lebanese cucumber
1 small red onion, grated
3 cups Greek-style, plain yoghurt
2 tbsp fresh mint, finely chopped
1 tsp dried dill
1 tbsp minced garlic
1 tsp salt
½ tsp black pepper
2 tbsp dried rose petals*

garnish
2 tbsp dried rose petals*
1 tbsp fresh mint, finely chopped

1   Peel and finely dice or grate the cucumber. Transfer to a serving dish with the grated onion.

2   Add the yoghurt and remaining ingredients and mix thoroughly. Garnish with the dried rose petals and finely chopped mint then refrigerate until needed.

serving suggestion
Serve with toasted lavash bread triangles as a dip, or as an accompaniment to a main meal.

note
*Dried rose petals are optional but give the dish a lovely, fragrant, fresh taste. They are available from Middle Eastern specialty shops.

Persian carpets

Carpet weaving is an integral part of Persian culture and art and dates back 2,500 years. Renowned for their richness in colour, superb quality and intricate patterns, they are indeed highly treasured possessions. Persian carpets can be found in palaces, famous buildings and museums all over the world.

آیس پک انار ، یا آنا، مین بار در ایران

jewelled salad

POMEGRANATE, MINT & CUCUMBER SALAD

1   Finely dice the cucumbers. Transfer to a serving bowl and add the spring onion, mint and pomegranate arils. Gently toss.

2   Mix together the dressing ingredients and drizzle over the salad just before serving.

serving suggestion
Serve chilled as a side dish.

note
*Sumac is a coarse, sour spice that can be found in Middle Eastern specialty shops.

serves 6   **prep** 10m   **cook** nil

2 Lebanese cucumbers
½ cup spring onion, thinly sliced
½ cup fresh mint, finely chopped
arils of 1 pomegranate

dressing
½ tsp minced garlic
1 tsp salt
½ tsp black pepper
pinch of sumac*
2 tbsp lime juice
1 tbsp olive oil

[pronounced / sab-zee mahk-loot]

sabzi mahkloot

FRESH HERB PLATTER WITH WALNUTS & FETTA

serves
6

prep
20m

cook
nil

fresh herbs
1 bunch mint
1 bunch coriander
1 bunch tarragon
1 bunch sweet basil
1 bunch flat leaf parsley
1 bunch chives

to serve
½ cup walnut halves
1 bunch radishes
1 bunch spring onion
100 g fetta cheese
flatbread

1   Wash and dry the herbs. Pinch off the leaves into small sections, discarding any thick stems, and toss the leaves together.

2   Place the walnuts in cold, salted water for 10 minutes. Strain, rinse and set aside.

3   Scrub the radishes. Cut off the roots and tops and slice thickly or serve whole. Wash and cut the spring onion into 10 cm lengths. Cut the fetta cheese into 2 cm cubes.

4   Arrange the mixed herbs, radishes, fetta cheese, spring onion and walnuts on a large platter. Refrigerate until needed.

serving suggestion
Serve with warmed flatbread as a delicious, healthy appetiser, or omit the fetta and walnuts and serve as an accompaniment to a main meal.

borani bademjoon

SMOKY EGGPLANT, GARLIC & YOGHURT DIP

1   Preheat the oven to 180 °C.

2   Place the eggplant on a gas burner over a high heat, occasionally turning, until the skin is blackened and charred. This step is optional but imparts a beautiful, smoky flavour to the eggplant. If omitting this step, prick the eggplant several times with a fork to prevent it bursting.

3   Wrap the eggplant in aluminium foil, place in an ovenproof dish and bake for 1 hour. Remove from the oven and allow to cool, before removing and discarding the blackened skin and mashing the flesh.

4   Heat the olive oil in a medium-sized, non-stick pan and fry the onion over a medium heat until golden-brown. Add the garlic and cook for another minute.

5   Add the mashed eggplant, liquid saffron, salt and pepper and simmer, covered for another 5 minutes, occasionally stirring. Remove from the heat and allow to cool to room temperature. Once cool, transfer to a serving dish and mix with the yoghurt. Garnish with the finely chopped mint and walnuts. Refrigerate for at least 30 minutes before serving.

serving suggestion
Serve as an appetiser, with vegetable sticks and crackers or warmed flatbread.

note
*See page 18 for instructions on how to make liquid saffron.

serves	prep	cook
6	5m	1h 15m

1 large eggplant
1 tbsp olive oil
1 large brown onion, finely chopped
2 tsp minced garlic, or 5 cloves
    baked garlic (see page 44)
1 tsp liquid saffron*
1 tsp salt
½ tsp black pepper
2 cups Greek-style, plain yoghurt

garnish
1 tbsp fresh mint, finely chopped
2 tbsp walnuts, finely chopped

The photos to the right are of the Azadi Tower (Freedom) and the surrounding views. It was built in commemoration of the 2,500th anniversary of the Persian Empire.

The impressive 50 metre structure was built in 1971 and stands at the gates of Tehran. The exterior is clad in 8000 precisely cut blocks of white marble, transported from the Esfahan province.

From the inside you can see the complex structural engineering, designed by architect Hossein Amanat. He won a competition to design a structure, which combines elements of pre- and post-Islamic architecture.

The Tower forms part of the Azadi cultural complex, located in Tehran's Azadi Square. At the base of the tower there is a beautiful park with several fountains and a museum underground.

[pronounced / zay-toon par-var-deh]

zeytoon parvardeh

OLIVES MARINATED IN POMEGRANATE, WALNUT & MINT

serves
6

prep
5m

marinate
4h

1 cup walnuts
4 tbsp olive oil
4 tbsp pomegranate purée*
2 tbsp verjuice**
2 tbsp minced garlic
½ cup fresh mint leaves
½ cup fresh coriander
1 tsp salt
½ tsp black pepper
1 tsp fennel seeds, ground
250 g pitted green olives

garnish
pomegranate arils
fresh mint leaves, torn

1   In a small, non-stick pan, dry roast the walnuts over a low to medium heat
for 5 minutes, constantly stirring. Remove from the heat and allow to cool,
before finely chopping in a food processor.

2   In a medium-sized bowl, mix the olive oil together with the pomegranate
purée, verjuice and minced garlic. Finely chop the mint leaves and coriander
and add to the mixture along with the chopped walnuts, salt, pepper, ground
fennel seeds and olives. Mix thoroughly.

3   Transfer to an airtight container and refrigerate for at least 4 hours and
up to 2 weeks. The longer you leave the olives to marinate, the more intense
the flavours become.

serving suggestion
Garnish with the pomegranate arils and torn mint leaves. Serve chilled.

notes
*Pomegranate purée is processed from the juice of a sour variety of
pomegranate. It can be found in Middle Eastern specialty shops.
**Verjuice is the juice of unripened grapes. It is not fermented, cooked, or
processed in any way. It is sour in taste, but milder than vinegar or lemon
juice. Verjuice can be found in Middle Eastern specialty shops.

Water, continuously
flowing from the
mountains high above,
keeps the doogh* cool
on the long, winding
road to Chaloos.

*Note: Doogh is a
traditional Iranian
drink made from yoghurt,
salt, water and a
little dried mint.

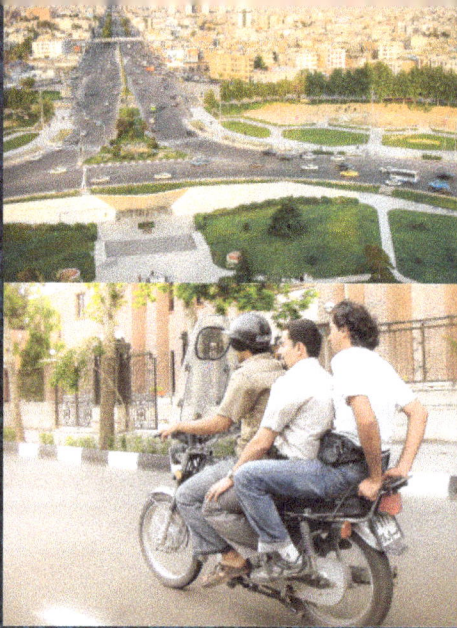

[pronounced / bo-raa-nee es-fan-aajh]

borani esfanaj

SPICED SPINACH & YOGHURT DIP

serves 6
prep 15m
cook 10m
chill 30m

1 bunch spinach
2 tsp olive oil
1 large brown onion, finely chopped
2 tsp minced garlic
½ tsp turmeric
½ tsp salt
1 tsp black pepper
½ tsp curry powder
1 tsp cumin
¼ tsp cinnamon
2 cups Greek-style, plain yoghurt

1   Wash the spinach thoroughly and pat dry.
Finely chop in a food processor and set aside.

2   Heat the olive oil in a medium-sized, non-stick
pan and fry the onion until golden-brown. Add the
garlic, turmeric, salt, pepper, curry powder, cumin
and cinnamon and fry for another 30 seconds.

3   Add the finely chopped spinach and continue
cooking over a low heat for another 5 minutes,
occasionally stirring.

4   Remove from the heat, transfer to a serving
dish and allow to cool.

5   Once cool, add the yoghurt, mix thoroughly
and place into the refrigerator for at least 30
minutes before serving.

serving suggestion

Serve as a dip with lavash bread triangles, or as
an accompaniment to a main meal.

quick tip

Frozen spinach can also be used to speed things up. Simply defrost, squeeze out any excess water and add at step 3.

baked garlic

For a milder tasting garlic, bake whole bulbs of garlic, with the skin on in a moderate oven for 30 minutes. Remove from the oven and allow to cool. Once cool, cut the tip from each clove and squeeze out the fleshy pulp.

mast musir

YOGHURT WITH WILD PERSIAN GARLIC

1   Place the dried musir pieces in a heatproof bowl and cover with boiling water. Set aside for 1 hour to soften, before straining and finely chopping.

2   Transfer the chopped musir to a serving bowl and mix together with the yoghurt, salt and pepper. Refrigerate for 30 minutes before serving.

serving suggestion
Serve as an accompaniment to a main meal, especially kebabs.

note
*Dried musir can be found in Middle Eastern specialty shops. It is a very mild-tasting garlic, that won't leave you with garlic breath. If you can't find musir, you can always substitute it for 2—3 cloves of baked garlic. See the recipe on page 44.

serves	prep	soak	chill
6	5m	1h	30m

12 dried musir pieces*
2 cups Greek-style, plain yogurt
1 tsp salt
½ tsp black pepper

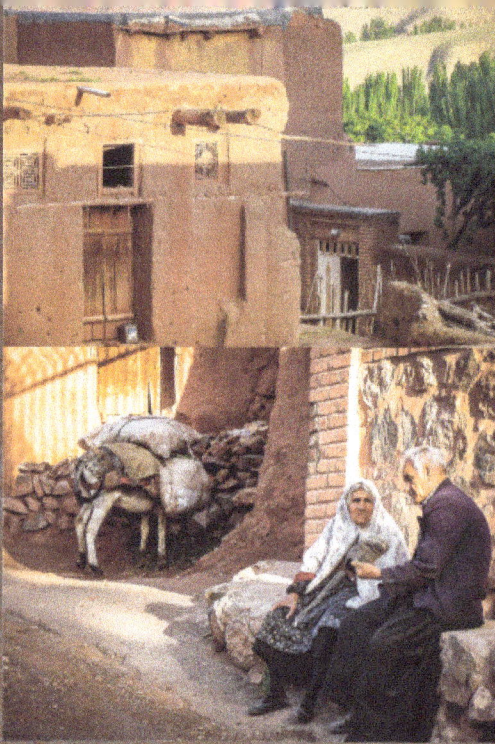

Pictured (left) is the 1,500 year-old, UNESCO-registered village of Abyaneh. It is one of the oldest villages in Iran and lies 70 km south of Kashan in the Esfahan province.

The permanent, although dwindling, population (mostly elderly) currently stands at 250.

The structures in the village are all made from clay, boasting a pinky-reddish colour and have gorgeous, worn, wooden doors.

The residents have persistently maintained their traditional costume. For women, this consists of a long, white scarf, with a colourful pattern, and, for men, black wide-legged trousers.

[pronounced / salad oh-liv-ee-yeh]

salad olivieh

PERSIAN CHICKEN & POTATO SALAD

serves
6

prep
15m

cook
2h 10m

10 large potatoes
4 cups (1 litre) water
1 whole chicken*
1 tbsp turmeric
1 tsp minced garlic
2 tsp salt
1 tsp black pepper
½ tsp cinnamon
6 eggs, hard boiled, finely
   chopped
200 g green gherkins, finely
   chopped
1 cup whole-egg mayonnaise

garnish
olives
cherry tomatoes

1   Preheat the oven to 200 °C. Individually wrap the unpeeled potatoes in aluminium foil and bake for 1 hour. Remove from the oven and allow to cool, before removing and discarding the skin and mashing the flesh.

2   Meanwhile, in a large pan, bring the water to the boil. Add the chicken, turmeric, garlic, 1 teaspoon of the salt, ½ teaspoon of the pepper and the cinnamon. Cover and simmer, over a low heat, for 2 hours. Remove the chicken from the liquid and allow to cool, before removing and discarding the skin and bones and breaking the white meat into small strips.

3   Transfer the mashed potato, chicken strips, chopped eggs and gherkins to a large bowl. Add the remaining teaspoon of salt and ½ teaspoon of pepper along with the mayonnaise, and mix thoroughly. You will probably need to get in with your hands, to ensure all ingredients are thoroughly combined.

4   Spoon the mixture onto a serving platter or dish and form into a mound. Use a spatula dipped in mayonnaise to smooth the surface and garnish with the olives and cherry tomatoes. Refrigerate until needed.

serving suggestion
Serve with fresh flatbread and pickles.

note
Salad olivieh will keep refrigerated for up to 3 days.

mirza ghassemi

SMOKY EGGPLANT WITH GARLIC, TOMATO & EGG

1   Preheat the oven to 180 °C.

2   Place the eggplant on a gas burner over a high heat, occasionally turning, until the skin is blackened and charred. This step is optional but imparts a beautiful, smoky flavour to the eggplant. If omitting this step, prick the eggplant several times with a fork to prevent it bursting.

3   Wrap the eggplant in aluminium foil, place in an ovenproof dish and bake for 1 hour. Remove from the oven and allow to cool, before removing and discarding the blackened skin and chopping the flesh into 1 cm cubes.

4   Heat the olive oil in a medium-sized, non-stick frying pan, and fry the onion over a medium heat until golden-brown. Add the garlic and the cooked eggplant, along with any juices, and continue to cook for another 5 minutes, stirring occasionally.

5   Add the salt, pepper, turmeric, curry powder and chilli flakes, and stir through the eggplant mixture. Add the tomatoes, tomato purée and liquid saffron. Stir briefly, cover and simmer over a low heat, for another 10 minutes.

6   Add the eggs and stir through until the mixture is thoroughly combined and the eggs are fully cooked.

serving suggestion
Serve warm, with plenty of fresh flatbread, Greek-style, plain yoghurt and fresh herbs. See page 34, for more information on fresh herbs.

note
*See page 18 for instructions on how to make liquid saffron.

serves	prep	cook
6	5m	1h 30m

1 large eggplant
2 tbsp olive oil
2 brown onions, finely chopped
2 tbsp minced garlic
1 tsp salt
½ tsp black pepper
1 tbsp turmeric
½ tsp curry powder
½ tsp dried chilli flakes
4 tomatoes, finely chopped
2 tbsp tomato purée
1 tsp liquid saffron*
4 eggs, beaten

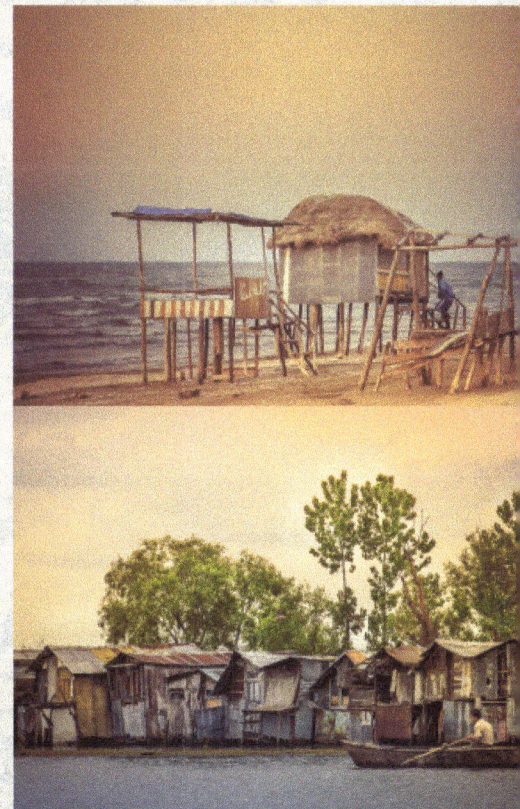

Mirza Ghassemi is a delicious dish originating from the Caspian Sea region in Iran.

The Caspian Sea is the largest, inland, enclosed body of water on earth, actually making it a lake. Ancient inhabitants of its coast perceived it to be an ocean, due to its saltiness and size.

Some of the best caviar in the world comes from the icy waters of the Caspian Sea. Here the environment is perfect for producing the finest sturgeon. Ninety per cent of the caviar produced in the world comes from the Caspian Sea.

salad shirazi

SHIRAZ CUCUMBER & TOMATO SALAD

1   Place the onion, tomato, cucumber, coriander and chilli in a large bowl and mix together. Refrigerate until needed.

2   Whisk the dressing ingredients together and add to the salad just before serving.

serves 6 **prep** 10m **cook** nil

1 red onion, finely diced
4 firm Roma tomatoes, finely diced
2 Lebanese cucumbers, finely diced
½ cup fresh coriander, finely chopped
1 red chilli, de-seeded, finely chopped

dressing
4 tbsp lime juice
2 tbsp olive oil
½ tsp minced garlic
½ tsp salt
½ tsp black pepper

[pronounced / kaa-hoo va sek-anj-e-been]

kahoo va sekanjebin

MINI COS LETTUCE WITH VINEGAR SYRUP

serves 6 | **prep** 5m | **cook** 1h | **chill** 30m

2 cups caster sugar
2 cups (500 ml) water
1½ cups (750 ml) white wine vinegar
6 sprigs fresh mint
2 strips lime rind
2 mini cos lettuce

1 In a small saucepan, mix the sugar and water together and gently heat until the sugar dissolves. Cover and simmer over a low heat for 10 minutes, occasionally stirring.

2 Add the vinegar and simmer for another 45 minutes, or until the mixture is thick and syrupy.

3 Remove from the heat, add the mint sprigs and lime rind and allow to cool to room temperature. Once cool, place into the refrigerator for 30 minutes.

4 Wash the lettuce, break into individual leaves and place on a large, flat tray. Remove the lime rind and mint from the cooled syrup and pour into a serving bowl.

serving suggestion
Serve the chilled syrup alongside the lettuce.

tasty tip

Kahoo va Sekanjebin is a delicious snack, perfect for a hot summer's day. The syrup can also be diluted with iced water for a refreshing, cooling drink.

dolmeh barg

STUFFED VINE LEAVES

1   In a small saucepan, bring 2 cups (500 ml) of water to the boil. Add the split peas and cook over a medium heat, for 10 minutes. Add the rice and cook for another 15 minutes. Strain under cold water and set aside.

2   Meanwhile, place the grape leaves in a large bowl, cover with boiling water and allow to stand for 5 minutes. Strain and set aside. This softens the leaves, making them easier to roll up. Line the bottom of large, wide pan, with damaged or torn grape leaves. This will prevent the dolmeh from sticking to the bottom of the pan.

3   In a large frying pan, heat the olive oil and fry the onion over a medium heat until golden-brown. Add the garlic and lamb mince and continue to cook until browned, stirring to break up any lumps.

4   Add the salt, pepper, curry powder, turmeric, advieh polo and cinnamon and fry for another 30 seconds. Remove the pan from the heat and add the dried rose petals, flat-leaf parsley, mint, dill, tarragon, melted butter and yoghurt along with the cooked split peas and rice. Stir gently to combine all the ingredients.

5   Take a single grape leaf and place vein side up on a chopping board. With a sharp knife, cut off the hard stem and place 1 tablespoon of the mixture onto the grape leaf. Fold the stem end over and then fold the sides in towards the centre. Continue to fold over again, to create a small square or roll and place seam side down into the prepared pan, on top of the unstuffed leaves. Repeat the process, arranging the rolled dolmeh in tight layers.

6   Once you have finished rolling, place a dinner plate over the top of the prepared dolmeh to weigh down and prevent them from unravelling while cooking.

7   Mix the sauce ingredients together and pour over the prepared dolmeh. Cover, and simmer gently for 2 hours. Remove the pan from the heat and allow the dolmeh cool, before transferring to a serving platter or container of your choice.

8   Mix together the garlic-lime yoghurt and refrigerate until required.

serving suggestion
These dolmeh are best served slightly warmed or at room temperature. Top with a drizzle of olive oil and serve with lemon wedges, the garlic lime yoghurt and fresh lavash bread. These dolmeh will keep for up to 1 week refrigerated or can be frozen for up to 3 months.

notes
*See page 20 for Persian spice blend for rice (advieh polo).
**Dried rose petals are optional but give the dish a lovely, fragrant, fresh taste. They are available from Middle Eastern specialty shops.
***See page 18 for instructions on how to make liquid saffron.

tip
Brined and prepackaged grape leaves can also be used, but be sure to rinse thoroughly under running water, to remove the excess salt.

makes 50   **prep** 45m   **cook** 2h

3 tbsp dried yellow split peas
¼ cup basmati rice
50 fresh grape leaves
4 tbsp olive oil
2 large brown onions, finely chopped
1 tbsp minced garlic
1 kg lamb mince
1 tsp salt
½ tsp black pepper
½ tsp curry powder
1 tbsp turmeric
1 tsp advieh polo*
½ tsp cinnamon
1 tbsp dried rose petals, crushed**
¼ cup fresh, flat-leaf parsley,
   finely chopped
1 tbsp fresh mint leaves,
   finely chopped
1 tbsp dried dill
1 tsp dried tarragon
¼ cup butter, melted
2 tbsp Greek style, plain yoghurt

sauce
4 tbsp olive oil
1 cup (250 ml) beef stock
¼ cup (60 ml) brown malt vinegar
2 tbsp lime juice
1 tsp liquid saffron***
½ tsp salt
½ tsp cinnamon

garlic-lime yoghurt
½ cup Greek-style, plain yoghurt
1 tsp minced garlic
1 tsp minced ginger
juice and zest of 1 lime

ash

Ash (pronounced osh) is a hearty soup laden with meat, grains, legumes, herbs and vegetables. Its consistency is, however, thicker than soup and is almost always served hot.

Ash is prepared relatively easily and inexpensively, but due to its delicate spice combinations, slow cooking and flavourful ingredients it becomes a rich, nourishing meal.

soups & breads

[pronounced / tuff-toon]

taftoon

PAN-FRIED FLATBREAD

makes	prep	prove	cook
8 loaves	20m	2h	5m/loaf

1½ cups (375 ml) warm water
7 g sachet active dry yeast
1 tsp sugar
3 cups white bread flour
1 cup wholemeal bread flour
1 tsp salt
pinch of turmeric
4 tbsp Greek-style, plain yoghurt

garnish
2 tbsp nigella seeds
2 tbsp sesame seeds

for cooking
2 tbsp olive oil

1   Pour half a cup (125 ml) of the warm water (approximately 45 °C) into a bowl and sprinkle the yeast and sugar over the top. Stir briefly, cover with a plate and set aside for 5 minutes. The yeast will dissolve in the water and you should now have a creamy, bubbling liquid.

2   Sift the flours into a large mixing bowl. Add the salt and turmeric and mix thoroughly.

3   Make a well in the centre of the flour and add the yeast mixture and yoghurt. Slowly add the rest of the warm water and continue mixing until the mixture becomes smooth and even. Transfer to a floured chopping board and continue to knead the mixture for 10 minutes.

4   Transfer the dough to a lightly oiled bowl, cover with a damp tea towel and leave to rise for 2 hours to double in size.

5   Lightly flour a chopping board. Transfer the dough to the board and firmly press down, with the heel of your hands, to knock the air out. With a sharp knife, evenly divide the dough into eight pieces and roll each piece into a ball.

6   Use a rolling pin to roll out each ball to a thin 20 cm circle. Use a fork to press a few holes in the dough and sprinkle with some nigella and sesame seeds.

7   Brush a little of the olive oil in a large, non-stick pan and heat the pan. Carefully transfer the rolled out dough to the pan and cook over a medium heat for 2—3 minutes per side.

8   Remove the loaf from the pan, cover with a tea towel and allow to cool. Continue to cook the remaining loaves.

tip
See the following page, for step-by-step, visual instructions.

dissolve yeast

sift flour

add liquids

beat 10 minutes

rise 2 hours

divide into eight

roll out

make holes

sprinkle seeds

traditional cooking in the tanoor oven

ash-e sholeh ghalamkar

BEGGAR'S SOUP

1   In a large soup pot, heat the oil and fry the onion over a medium heat until golden-brown. Add the garlic and cook for another minute. Add the lamb bones and brown all over.

2   Add the water, salt, pepper, turmeric, cinnamon and mint to the pot and bring to the boil. Cover and simmer for 2 hours, over a low heat or until the meat is fully cooked.

3   With a slotted spoon, remove the meat from the pot, let cool slightly and pound with a mortar and pestle, removing any bones as you go. Return the meat to the pot and add the black-eyed beans, rice, and green lentils.

4   Rinse and strain the kidney beans and add along with the dill and finely chopped herbs. Cover and simmer over a low heat for another 2 hours, stirring occasionally.

5   Meanwhile, prepare the garnish. Heat the olive oil in a medium-sized, non-stick pan and fry the onion until golden-brown. Add the garlic and cook for another minute. Sprinkle the mint and turmeric over the onions and garlic, stir briefly then remove the pan from the heat.

serving suggestion

Ladle into individual serving bowls and decorate with the fried onion mixture. Serve hot, with warmed flatbread and lemon wedges.

serves 6 | **prep** 20m | **cook** 4h

2 tbsp canola oil
2 large brown onions,
   finely chopped
1 tbsp minced garlic
500 g lamb soup bones
10 cups (2.5 litres) water
1 tsp salt
½ tsp black pepper
1 tbsp turmeric
1 tsp cinnamon
½ tsp dried mint
½ cup dried black-eyed beans
½ cup basmati rice
½ cup dried green lentils
420 g can red kidney beans
3 tbsp dried dill
½ cup fresh, flat-leaf parsley,
   finely chopped
½ cup coriander, finely chopped
½ cup spinach, finely chopped
½ cup spring onion,
   finely chopped

garnish
2 tbsp olive oil
1 large brown onion, finely sliced
1 tbsp minced garlic
1 tbsp dried mint
1 tsp turmeric

to serve
lemon wedges
fresh flatbread

soup-e jo

CREAM OF BARLEY SOUP

serves 6

prep 10m

cook 1h 40m

2 tbsp canola oil
2 large brown onions, finely chopped
1 leek, finely chopped
1 tsp minced garlic
½ cup pearl barley
6 cups (1.5 litres) chicken stock
1 tsp salt
½ tsp black pepper
½ tsp turmeric
½ cup button mushrooms
1 carrot, grated
½ cup sour cream
2 tbsp lime juice
2 tbsp lime zest

garnish
2 tsp flat-leaf parsley, finely chopped
2 tbsp lime zest

to serve
limes, halved
flatbread

1   In a large soup pot, heat the oil and fry the onion over a medium heat until golden-brown. Add the leek and garlic and cook for another 5 minutes.

2   Add the barley, chicken stock, salt, pepper and turmeric. Cover and simmer over a low heat for 1 hour, stirring occasionally.

3   Finely slice the mushrooms and add to the pot along with the grated carrot. Simmer for another 30 minutes.

4   In a small bowl, mix together ½ cup of the soup with the sour cream. Add to the soup and stir through briefly. Remove the pan from the heat, add the lime juice and zest and stir through.

serving suggestion
Ladle into individual serving bowls and garnish with the parsley and lime zest. Serve hot, with warmed flatbread and a squeeze of lime juice.

[pronounced / ad-as-see]

adasi

LENTIL SOUP

1   In a medium-sized soup pot, heat the oil and fry the onion over a medium heat until golden-brown.

2   Wash and rinse the lentils and add to the onion, along with the spices. Stir briefly, add the water and lime juice and bring to the boil. Once boiling, lower the heat to minimum, cover and simmer for 1 hour or until the lentils are tender, stirring occasionally.

3   You can serve the lentils just as they are, or you can blend half of the soup, return to the pan and continue to cook until just heated through.

serving suggestion

Ladle into individual serving bowls. Serve hot with a little extra lime juice or vinegar and fresh flatbread.

serves 6 | **prep** 5m | **cook** 1h 10m

2 tsp canola oil
2 large brown onions,
   finely chopped
2 cups dried, green lentils
1 tsp salt
½ tsp black pepper
¼ tsp cinnamon
2 tbsp turmeric
6 cups (1.5 litres) water
4 tbsp lime juice

to serve
dash of lime juice,
   or vinegar
warmed flatbread

Adasi is often served at the Persian breakfast table. The photo to the right is, however, a more typical Persian breakfast.

Breakfast usually consists of warmed barbari, sangak or taftoon bread. Accompaniments include: fresh cream and butter with honey and jams or fetta cheese with sliced tomato and cucumber.

Boiled eggs and omelettes are also quite popular.

Of course, no Persian breakfast would be complete without freshly brewed, strong, black tea.

mini barbari

MINI THICK FLATBREADS

makes
4 loaves

prep
20m

prove
2h 30m

cook
30m

1¼ cups (310 ml) warm water
7 g sachet active dry yeast
1 tsp sugar
3½ cups white bread flour
1 tsp salt
pinch of turmeric

garnish
2 tbsp sesame seeds
2 tbsp nigella seeds

glaze
1 tsp bicarbonate of soda
1 tsp white flour
½ cup (125 ml) water

1   Pour half a cup (125 ml) of the warm water (approximately 45 °C) into a small bowl. Sprinkle the yeast and sugar over the top, stir briefly and cover with a plate. Set aside for 5 minutes. The yeast will dissolve in the water, and you should now have a creamy, bubbling liquid.

2   Sift the flour into a large mixing bowl. Add the salt and turmeric and mix thoroughly.

3   Make a well in the centre of the flour, add the yeast mixture and mix well. Slowly add the rest of the warm water and continue mixing until the mixture becomes smooth and even.

4   Transfer the dough to a floured chopping board and knead the mixture for 10 minutes.

5   Lightly oil a large bowl and transfer the dough to the bowl. Cover with cling film and a plate and leave to rise for 2 hours, or until doubled in size.

6   Transfer the dough to a lightly floured chopping board and press down with the heel of your palms to knock the air out. With a sharp knife, evenly divide the dough into four pieces and roll each piece into a ball.

7   Use a rolling pin to roll out each ball into a long, oval shape approximately 2 cm thick. Cover with the damp tea towel and allow to rise for another 30 minutes.

8   Meanwhile make the glaze. Mix the bicarbonate of soda, white flour and water together in a small saucepan and bring to the boil. Set aside to cool.

9   Preheat oven the to 170 °C. Transfer the loaves to a lightly greased tray lined with baking paper. Using a wet finger, make four vertical lines down the length of each loaf. Brush the top of each loaf with the prepared glaze and sprinkle with some nigella and sesame seeds. Place the tray on the lowest shelf of the oven and bake for 30 minutes.

tip

If you have a pizza stone, it will be to your advantage to preheat and use it. Barbari should be crisp on the bottom and fluffy inside.

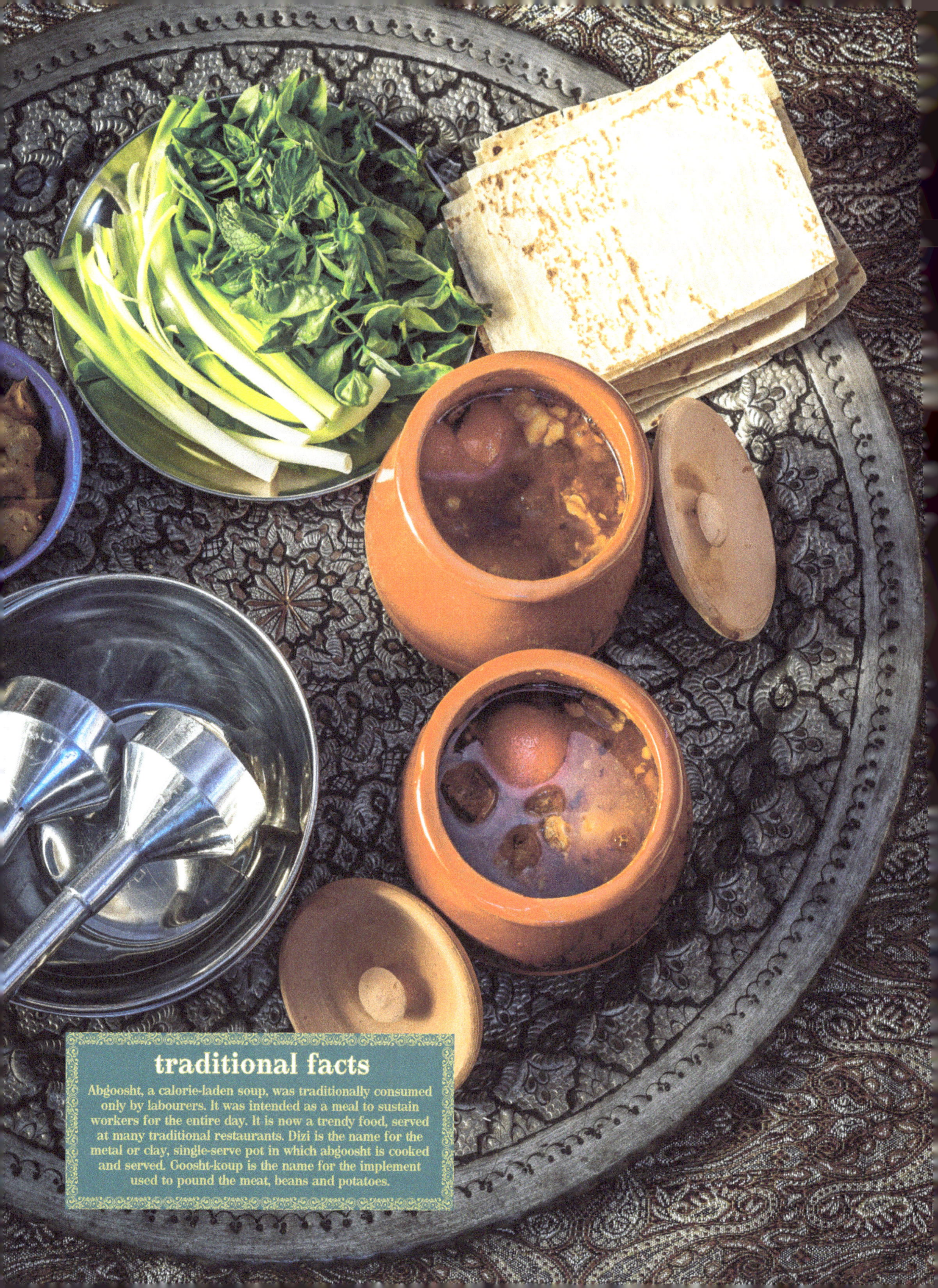

abgoosht

[pronounced / ob-goosh-t]

TWO-PART LAMB & POTATO BROTH WITH CHICKPEAS

1 With a sharp knife, remove as much lamb meat from the bone as possible. Cut the meat into 2—3cm cubes. Heat the oil in a large, heavy-based pan and fry the lamb, including any bones, in small batches until browned all over. Remove from the pan with a slotted spoon, set aside and continue cooking the remainder of the lamb.

2 Add a little more oil to the pan if necessary and fry the onion over a medium heat, until golden-brown. Add the garlic and cook for another minute. Return the lamb and bones to the pan, add the water and bring to the boil.

3 Pierce the dried limes with a fork several times and add to the pan along with the turmeric, tomato purée, liquid saffron, salt, pepper and cinnamon. Rinse and strain the chick peas and add to the pan along with the dried white beans. Reduce the heat to minimum, cover and simmer over a low heat for 3 hours.

4 Add the potatoes and tomatoes, and continue to simmer over a low heat for another hour.

serving suggestion

Part 1: Pour or ladle the liquid part of the soup into individual serving bowls. Serve the broth with day-old lavash bread, which everyone can then tear into small pieces and throw in their soup.

Part 2: Separate the bones from the meat and mash the remaining ingredients together to form a smooth, thick paste. Serve the mash now with the fresh lavash bread, spring onion, fresh herbs and pickles.

notes

*Dried limes are available from Middle Eastern speciality shops. They impart a delicious, sour, tart taste to dishes. They can be left in the food and eaten or removed prior to serving. If you can't source them, you can substitute with 1—2 teaspoons of lime juice.
**See page 18 for instructions on how to make liquid saffron.
***See page 34 for suitable types of fresh herbs.

serves | prep | cook
6 | 10m | 4h

500 g lamb leg, with bone
2 tsp canola oil
2 large brown onions, finely chopped
1 tsp minced garlic
10 cups (2.5 litres) water
4 dried limes*
3 tbsp turmeric
1 tbsp tomato purée
1 tsp liquid saffron**
1 tbsp salt
½ tsp black pepper
½ tsp cinnamon
425 g can chickpeas
1 cup dried white beans
6 small potatoes, halved
6 small tomatoes, halved

to serve
day-old lavash bread
fresh lavash bread
spring onion
fresh herbs***

ash-e jo

HEARTY BARLEY SOUP

serves 6 | **prep** 20m | **cook** 2h

4 cups (1 litre) beef stock
4 cups (1 litre) water
1 tsp salt
½ tsp black pepper
½ tsp cinnamon
1 tbsp turmeric
1 cup dried green lentils
¼ cup basmati rice
1 cup pearl barley
420 g can red kidney beans
420 g can chickpeas
1 cup fresh, flat-leaf parsley,
    finely chopped
1 cup spinach, finely chopped
1 cup fresh chives, finely
    chopped
2 tbsp dried dill
1 cup fresh coriander, finely
    chopped
¼ cup sour cream

garnish
2 tbsp olive oil
1 large brown onion, finely
    sliced
1 tsp turmeric
2 tbsp minced garlic
1 tbsp dried mint

to serve
sour cream
flatbread

1   In a large soup pot, bring the beef stock and water to the boil. Add the salt, pepper, cinnamon and turmeric along with the lentils, rice and barley. Stir briefly and simmer, covered, over a low heat for 1 hour, stirring occasionally.

2   Meanwhile prepare the garnish. Heat the olive oil in a small, non-stick pan and fry the onion over a medium heat until golden-brown. Sprinkle the turmeric over the onions and stir briefly. Remove the onions from the pan and set aside. Reheat the pan, adding a little more oil if necessary and fry the garlic for 30 seconds over a low heat. Sprinkle the mint on top, stir briefly, remove from the heat and set aside.

3   Strain and rinse the kidney beans and chickpeas. Add to the pot along with the parsley, spinach, chives, dill and coriander. Cover and continue to cook for another hour or until all ingredients are tender. Stir occasionally, to prevent the ingredients from sticking to the bottom of the pot.

4   In a small bowl, mix half a cup of the soup with the sour cream. Add to the soup, stir through briefly then remove from the heat.

serving suggestion
Ladle into individual bowls and decorate with the fried onion, garlic and mint and a little extra sour cream. Serve with warmed flatbread.

[pronounced / osh-e mosst]

ash-e mast

YOGHURT & HERB SOUP WITH LAMB MEATBALLS

1 Heat the oil in a large soup pot and fry the onion over a medium heat until golden-brown. Add the garlic and cook for another minute. Add the salt, pepper and water and bring to the boil.

2 Add the rice, lentils and chickpeas, cover, and simmer over a low heat for 30 minutes.

3 Meanwhile, make the meatballs. Thoroughly combine the six ingredients and form into small balls, the size of hazelnuts.

4 Add the meatballs to the pot, along with the spinach, coriander and dill, cover and simmer over a low heat for another hour.

5 Meanwhile, prepare the garnish. Heat the olive oil in a small, non-stick pan and fry the onion over a medium heat until golden-brown. Add the garlic and cook for another minute. Sprinkle the mint and turmeric on top, stir briefly, remove from the heat and set aside.

6 Mix the yoghurt together with 1 cup of the hot soup and add to the pan. Simmer, uncovered, over the lowest heat setting for 5 minutes, stirring constantly.

serving suggestion
Ladle into individual serving bowls. Garnish with the fried onion mixture.

variation
As a vegetarian option, simply omit the meatballs.

tip
It is important to have the yoghurt brought to room temperature for this recipe, to prevent it curdling.

serves
6

prep
10m

cook
1h 45m

2 tbsp canola oil
2 large brown onions, finely chopped
1 tsp minced garlic
1½ tsp salt
½ tsp black pepper
6 cups (1.5 litres) water
½ cup basmati rice
420 g can brown lentils
420 g can chickpeas
½ cup spinach, finely chopped
½ cup fresh coriander, finely chopped
2 tbsp dried dill
2 cups Greek-style, plain yoghurt, brought to room temperature

meatballs
250 g lamb mince
1 small brown onion, grated
½ cup breadcrumbs
½ tsp salt
½ tsp black pepper
½ tsp cinnamon

garnish
2 tbsp olive oil
1 large brown onion, finely sliced
1 tbsp minced garlic
1 tbsp dried mint
1 tsp turmeric

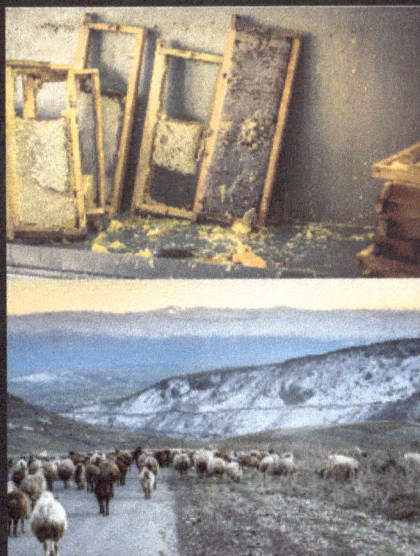

The photos to the left were taken in Sarein, located in the centre of the Ardabil province in the north of Iran.

Sarein is famous for its dairy products, produced from the local sheep and cows. The thick clotted cream in Sarein, called Sar Shir, meaning top of the milk, is absolutely out of this world. Honey and mineral hot springs are also famous in Sarein. The hot springs are thanks to Mt Sabalon, an inactive volcano with a height of 4,800 metres.

The cooler climate of Sarein and the rich mineral soil mean the sheep and cattle always have an abundance of rich, green pastures.

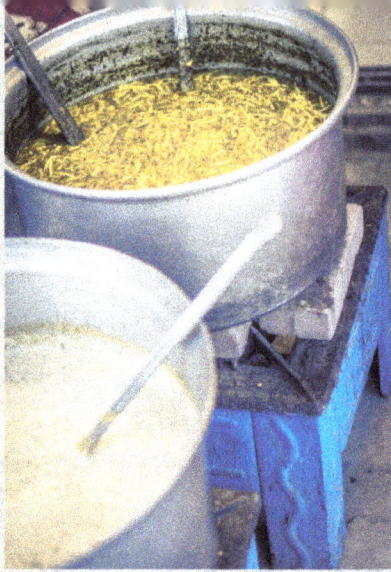

Ash-e reshteh always makes an appearance during the Persian Nowruz celebrations. The noodles symbolise the unraveling of life's problems. Nowruz, is the traditional festival of the start of spring and is considered as the beginning of a new year.

Prior to Nowruz folk clean their houses from top to bottom, buy new clothes, get their hair cut and so on.

[pronounced / osh-e resh-teh]

ash-e reshteh

HERB, BEAN & NOODLE SOUP WITH LAMB MEATBALLS

serves 6 | **prep** 20m | **cook** 2h 30m

2 tsp canola oil
2 large brown onions, finely chopped
1 tsp minced garlic
2 tbsp turmeric, heaped
1 tsp salt
½ tsp black pepper
8 cups (2 litres) water
½ cup dried, black-eyed beans
½ cup dried, green lentils
425 g can red kidney beans
425 g can chickpeas
2 tbsp brown, malt vinegar
½ cup fresh, flat-leaf parsley,
  finely chopped
½ cup spinach, finely chopped
2 tbsp dried dill
2 cups reshteh noodles*
  or capellini pasta
½ cup sour cream

meatballs
500 g lamb mince
1 small brown onion, grated
½ cup breadcrumbs
1 tsp salt
½ tsp black pepper
½ tsp cinnamon

garnish
2 tbsp olive oil
1 large brown onion, finely sliced
1 tbsp minced garlic
1 tbsp dried mint
1 tsp turmeric
½ tsp cinnamon

1   Heat the oil in a large soup pot and fry the onion over a medium heat until golden-brown. Add the garlic and cook for another minute. Add the turmeric, salt, pepper and water and bring to the boil. Add the black-eyed beans and green lentils, cover and simmer over a low heat for 1 hour.

2   Meanwhile, make the meatballs. Thoroughly combine the 6 ingredients and form into small balls, the size of hazelnuts.

3   Strain and rinse the red kidney beans and chickpeas. Add to the pot along with the vinegar, parsley, spinach and dill. Carefully add the meatballs, cover and simmer over low heat for another 45 minutes.

4   Break the reshteh noodles into 6 centimetre lengths and add to the soup. Simmer uncovered over low heat for an additional 45 minutes, stirring frequently. Note: It may be necessary at this point to add a little extra water if required.

5   Meanwhile, prepare the garnish. Heat the olive oil in a small, non-stick pan and fry the onion over a medium heat until golden-brown. Add the garlic and cook for another minute. Sprinkle the mint, turmeric and cinnamon on top, stir briefly, remove from the heat and set aside.

6   Mix the sour cream together with half a cup of the hot soup and add to the pan. Simmer uncovered, until just heated through.

serving suggestion
Ladle into individual serving bowls. Garnish with the fried onion mixture and a swirl of sour cream.

note
*See page 16 for more information on reshteh noodles.

vegetarian option

Ash-e reshteh can also be served as a delicious vegetarian meal. Simply omit the meatball ingredients and skip step 2 in the method.

kookoo

Kookoo is a versatile, easy to make dish, similar to frittata. The ingredients are predominantly eggs, vegetables, fresh herbs and occasionally meat.

It is often served as a light meal with flatbread, yoghurt and pickles. It can also be cut into small pieces and served as an entrée or appetiser.

light meals

82 **kookoo sabzi**
fresh herb frittata

85 **ghormeh sabzi pizza**
fresh herb pizza

86 **halim bademjoon**
lamb, lentil & eggplant purée

89 **kookoo goosht**
mini lamb & spinach frittatas

dolmeh kalam 90
lamb & herb stuffed cabbage leaves

dolmeh bademjoon, felfel va gojeh farangi 94
stuffed eggplants, capsicums & tomatoes

kookoo joojeh 96
chicken frittata

kookoo bademjoon 100
eggplant frittata

If you don't have a frying pan with a removable or heatproof handle, you can use an ordinary frying pan for the first 5 stages. At stage 6, place a flat tray, larger than your pan, over the top of the kookoo and carefully flip the pan over. Note: You need to take great care at this stage to avoid serious burns from the hot oil. After this, simply reheat the pan with the remaining butter, and slide the kookoo back in.

Left photo: Fresh barberries

[pronounced / koo-koo sab-zee]

kookoo sabzi

FRESH HERB FRITTATA

serves 8   **prep** 15m   **cook** 30m

1 leek, green ends only
1 cup fresh, flat-leaf parsley
2 cups spinach
1 cup fresh coriander leaves
1 cup celery leaves
2 tbsp dried dill
1½ tbsp flour
1 tbsp fenugreek seeds, ground*
2 tbsp barberries**
8 eggs
1 tsp salt
½ tsp black pepper
½ tsp cinnamon
½ tsp turmeric
2 tbsp minced garlic

for cooking
¼ cup canola oil
2 tbsp butter, melted

1   Preheat the oven to 180 ˚C.

2   Thoroughly wash the leek, parsley, spinach, coriander and celery leaves and pat dry. Finely chop in a food processor then transfer to a large mixing bowl.

3   Add the dill, flour, the ground fenugreek seeds and barberries and mix well.

4   In a separate bowl, lightly beat the eggs. Add the salt, pepper, cinnamon, turmeric and garlic and mix well. Add to the chopped vegetables and stir to combine.

5   In a deep-sided frying pan with a removable or heatproof handle, heat the canola oil and 1 tablespoon of the butter until hot. Carefully pour in the mixture and cook, uncovered, over a medium heat for 15 minutes.

6   Remove the pan from the heat and pour the remaining melted butter over the surface of the frittata and place in the oven. Cook for 15 minutes. Check to see if ready by piercing the centre with a skewer. If it comes out clean, it is cooked.

serving suggestion
Cut into eight, even-sized pieces. Serve warm or cold with fresh flatbread, yoghurt and pickles.

notes
*Fenugreek seeds have a slightly bitter, curry-like flavour. They are hard, oval seeds, about 3 mm in length. They should be ground before use.
**Barberries have a delicious, tart, sour taste. They are available from Middle Eastern specialty shops. If you can't find them you can omit from the recipe.

tip

This recipe makes great use of leftover ghormeh sabzi (see recipe on page 104). You'll need half a cup. Canned ghormeh sabzi without meat is also available from Middle Eastern speciality shops.

ghormeh sabzi pizza

FRESH HERB PIZZA

1   Pour half a cup (125 ml) of the warm water (approximately 45 °C) into a bowl and sprinkle the yeast and sugar over the top. Stir briefly and cover with a plate. Set aside for 5 minutes. The yeast will dissolve into the water, and you should now have a creamy, bubbling liquid.

2   Sift the flour into a large mixing bowl. Add the salt and mix thoroughly. Make a well in the centre, pour in the yeast mixture and olive oil and stir to combine. Slowly add the rest of the warm water (250 ml) and continue mixing until the mixture becomes smooth and even. Transfer to a floured chopping board and continue to knead the mixture for 10 minutes.

3   Transfer the dough to a lightly oiled bowl, cover with cling film and a plate, and leave to rise for 2 hours, or until doubled in size.

4   Meanwhile, prepare the mincemeat topping. In a large, non-stick pan heat the oil and fry the onion over a medium heat until golden-brown. Add the garlic and ginger and cook for another minute.

5   Add the lamb mince and continue to cook until the meat has browned, stirring to break up any lumps. Add the salt, pepper, turmeric, tomato purée and water. Simmer uncovered over a low heat for 10 minutes, or until very little liquid remains. Remove from the heat and set aside.

6   Lightly flour a chopping board, transfer the dough and press down with the heel of your hands to knock the air out. With a sharp knife, evenly divide the dough into two pieces and roll each piece into a ball.

7   Use a rolling pin to roll out each ball to a thin 30 cm circle. Use a fork to prick a few holes in the dough and set aside for 10 minutes.

8   Preheat oven the to 210 °C. Prepare the pizzas by first spreading with a thin layer of tomato purée. Next evenly spread with the mincemeat topping and finally the pre-made ghormeh sabzi sauce. Bake in the oven for 20 minutes.

note
*The recipe for ghormeh sabzi can be found on page 104.

makes | prep | prove | cook
2 large | 20m | 2h | 30m

pizza dough
1½ cups (375 ml) warm water
7 g sachet active dried yeast
1 tsp caster sugar
4 cups plain flour
1 tsp salt
4 tbsp olive oil

mincemeat topping
2 tbsp canola oil
1 large brown onion, finely chopped
½ tsp minced garlic
½ tsp minced ginger
250 g lamb mince
1 tsp salt
½ tsp black pepper
½ tsp turmeric
1 tbsp tomato purée
½ cup (125 ml) water

other toppings
2 tbsp tomato purée
½ cup pre-made ghormeh sabzi
Mozzarella cheese (optional)

The creator of the ghormeh sabzi pizza is an Iranian chef. A few years ago he won first place in a pizza making competition in Italy out of 450 other contestants.

You can see in the fruit and vegetable markets in Iran an abundant supply of fresh herbs at what appears to be very cheap prices.

Iranians eat fresh herbs with almost every meal, and also cook and freeze them for later use, when they are out of season.

[pronounced / hal-eem bod-em-joon]

halim bademjoon

LAMB, LENTIL & EGGPLANT PURÉE

serves 6   **prep** 15m   **cook** 4h

1 large eggplant
2 tbsp olive oil
2 large brown onions,
    finely chopped
1 tsp minced garlic
500 g stewing lamb, with bone
½ tsp salt
½ tsp black pepper
½ tsp turmeric
1 cup green lentils
6 cups (1.5 litres) water
2 tbsp sour cream

garnish
4 tbsp olive oil
1 onion, finely sliced
2 tbsp minced garlic
1 tbsp dried mint

to serve
2 tbsp sour cream
2 tsp liquid saffron*
flatbread
fresh herbs**

1   Preheat the oven to 180 °C.

2   Place the eggplant on a gas burner over a high heat, occasionally turning, until the skin is blackened and charred. This step is optional but imparts a beautiful, smoky flavour to the eggplant. If omitting this step, prick the eggplant several times, with a fork to prevent it bursting in the oven.

3   Wrap the eggplant in aluminium foil, place in an ovenproof dish and bake for 1 hour. Remove from the oven and allow to cool, before removing and discarding the blackened skin and mashing the flesh.

4   Meanwhile, in a large, non-stick pan, heat the oil and fry the onion over a medium heat until golden-brown. Add the garlic and lamb and brown on all sides.

5   Add the salt, pepper, turmeric and water, cover and simmer over a low heat, for 2 hours. Remove the pan from the heat and allow to cool slightly. Remove the meat from the pan with a slotted spoon and discard the bones.

6   Return the meat to the pan and place back on the heat. Add the lentils and eggplant, cover and simmer over a low heat for another 2 hours. Remove from the heat and allow to cool slightly.

7   Meanwhile, prepare the garnish. Heat the olive oil in a non-stick pan and fry the onion over a medium heat until golden-brown. Add the garlic and cook for another minute. Sprinkle the mint on top, stir and continue cooking. As soon as the aroma of mint arises, remove from the heat.

8   Use a hand-held blender or mixer to purée the lamb, lentils and eggplant mixture. Add the sour cream and stir through. Return the pan to the heat until just heated through.

serving suggestion
Spoon the purée onto a flat dish or tray. Top with the sour cream, fried onion mixture and a drizzle of liquid saffron. Serve with fresh flatbread and plenty of fresh herbs**.

notes
*See page 18 for instructions on how to make liquid saffron.
**See page 34 for information on suitable types of fresh herbs.

[pronounced / koo-koo goo-sht]

kookoo goosht

MINI LAMB & SPINACH FRITTATAS

1   Preheat the oven to 180 °C. Grease eight ramekins or an eight-pan muffin tray.

2   In a large frying pan, heat the olive oil and fry the onion over a medium heat until golden-brown. Add the lamb mince and garlic and continue to cook until the meat has browned, stirring to break up any lumps.

3   Add the salt, pepper, curry powder, turmeric and cinnamon and stir briefly. Remove from the heat, add the flour, spinach and leek. Mix well.

4   Lightly beat the eggs and add to the meat mixture. Stir to thoroughly combine all ingredients. Spoon into the ramekins or muffin tray. Fill to 1 cm below the top and bake for 20 minutes. Check to see if ready by piercing the centre with a skewer. If it comes out clean, it is cooked.

serving suggestion
Serve warm, topped with yoghurt and finely sliced spring onion.

makes 8 | **prep** 10m | **cook** 30m

2 tbsp olive oil
1 large onion, finely chopped
250 g lamb mince
1 tsp minced garlic
1½ tsp salt
½ tsp black pepper
1 tsp curry powder
1 tsp turmeric
½ tsp cinnamon
1 tbsp flour
1 cup spinach, finely chopped
½ cup leek, finely chopped
8 eggs

garnish
2 tbsp Greek-style, plain yoghurt
2 tbsp spring onion, finely sliced

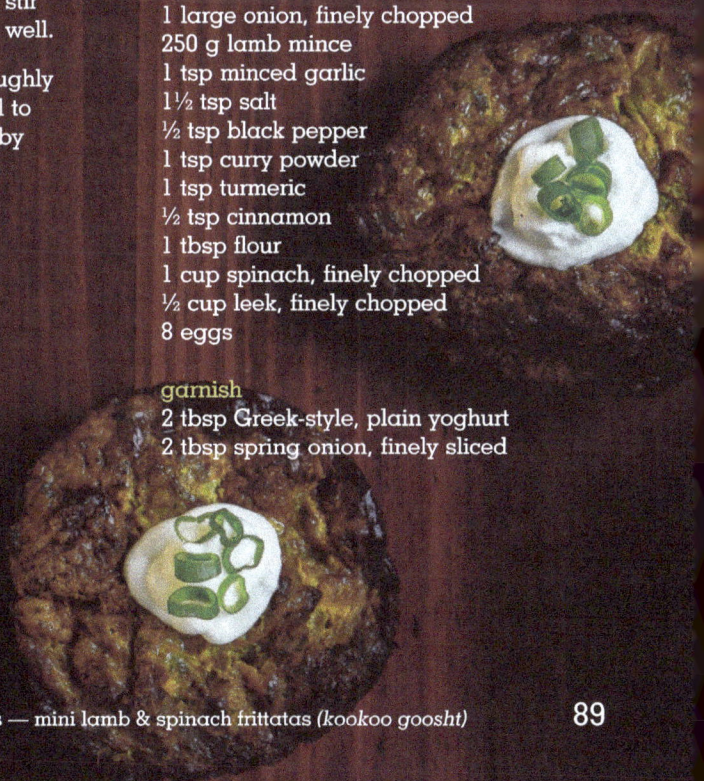

dolmeh kalam

LAMB & HERB STUFFED CABBAGE LEAVES

serves 6   **prep** 1h   **cook** 3h

2 tbsp canola oil
1 large brown onion, finely chopped
1 tsp minced garlic
500 g diced lamb, cut into
   ½ cm cubes
1 tsp turmeric
1 tsp salt
½ tsp black pepper
¼ tsp cinnamon
3 cups (750 ml) water
2 tbsp tomato purée
½ cup basmati rice
1 large green cabbage
¼ cup fresh, flat-leaf parsley,
   finely chopped
2 tbsp dried mint
1 tbsp dried dill
1 tbsp dried tarragon

sauce
2 cups (500 ml) water
3 tbsp tomato purée
¼ cup (60 ml) vinegar, or
   2 tbsp lemon juice
2 tbsp olive oil
½ tsp salt
½ tsp black pepper
½ tsp minced garlic

1   In a large, non-stick pan heat the oil and fry the onion over a medium heat until golden-brown. Add the garlic and cook for another minute. Add the cubed lamb and brown all over. Add the turmeric, salt, pepper and cinnamon and stir briefly. Add the water and tomato purée and bring to the boil. Cover and simmer over a low heat for 1½ hours, or until the meat is fully cooked and very little liquid remains.

2   Meanwhile, in a small saucepan bring 2 cups (500 ml) of water to the boil, add the rice and cook for 5—7 minutes. The rice should be soft on the outside, but not fully cooked. Strain, rinse under cool water and set aside.

3   Fill a large, deep sided pan with 6 cups (1.5 litres) of water and bring to the boil. Meanwhile, cut around the core of the cabbage, remove and discard. Remove and discard any outer torn leaves and place the cabbage core side up into the boiling water. Cover and simmer gently for 5 minutes before straining and rinsing under cool water. Once the cabbage has cooled slightly, remove individual leaves, being careful not to tear them as you go. With a sharp knife, cut out any thick, hard centre-ribs from the leaves as necessary.

4   Once the meat is cooked, remove the pan from the heat and add the parboiled rice, parsley, mint, dill and tarragon. Gently mix to combine.

5   Take a medium-sized pan, with a lid, and line the bottom with any torn cabbage leaves.

6   Place an individual cabbage leaf on the chopping board, concave side up, with the core facing towards you. Take a heaped tablespoon of the meat mixture and place near the edge of the leaf. Roll over this end, then roll the two sides towards the centre. Continue to roll up and place each dolmeh seam-side down in the pan. Place them tightly together and in a single layer.

7   Mix the sauce ingredients together and pour over the dolmeh. Place a dinner plate on top of the dolmeh to weigh them down. Cover and simmer over a low heat, for 1½ hours.

serving suggestion
Serve hot, drizzled with the sauce, fresh flatbread and yoghurt.

remove core

boil 5 minutes

remove leaves

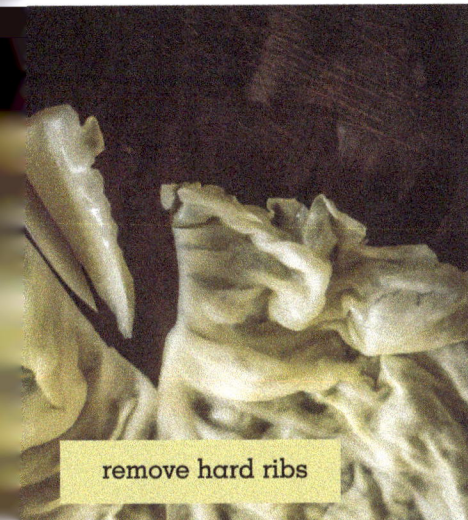

remove hard ribs

line pan

add filling

roll over end

roll in left side

roll in right side

roll up

place in pan

pour over sauce

ðolmeh baðemjoon, felfel va gojeh farangi

STUFFED EGGPLANTS, CAPSICUMS & TOMATOES

serves
6

prep
20m

cook
2h 30m

2 small eggplants
2 yellow capsicums
2 large tomatoes

stuffing
½ cup yellow split peas
½ cup basmati rice
2 tbsp olive oil
1 large brown onion, finely
    chopped
1 tsp minced garlic
500 g lamb mince
1 tsp salt
½ tsp black pepper
½ tsp cinnamon
1 tbsp turmeric
½ cup (125 ml) water
½ cup fresh, flat-leaf parsley,
    finely chopped
½ cup fresh coriander, finely
    chopped
½ cup spinach, finely chopped
2 tbsp dried mint
1 tbsp dried tarragon

sauce
1 tsp liquid saffron*
½ cup tomato purée
1½ cups (375 ml) water
3 tbsp lemon juice
1 tsp salt
½ tsp black pepper

1   Cut off the stem tops from the eggplants, capsicums and tomatoes, and save. Scoop the insides out from the eggplants and tomatoes, leaving about 1 cm of flesh. Take care not to break the outer layer. Scrape the seeds and white membrane from the capsicums.

2   In a small saucepan, bring 2 cups (500 ml) of water to the boil. Add the split peas and cook for over a medium heat for 10 minutes. Add the rice and continue to cook for another 15 minutes. Strain under cool water and set aside.

3   Meanwhile, in a medium-sized, non-stick pan, heat the oil and fry the onion over a medium heat, until golden-brown. Add the garlic and cook for another minute.

4   Add the lamb mince, stir to break up any lumps and brown slightly. Add the salt, pepper, cinnamon, turmeric and water. Simmer uncovered over a low heat for 10 minutes, or until very little liquid remains.

5   Add the pre-cooked split peas and rice to the lamb mince, along with the remaining chopped and dried herbs. Mix well and remove from the heat. Fill the eggplants, capsicums and tomatoes with the mixture. Put the saved stem tops back on, and fasten with toothpicks. Place the eggplants and capsicums upright, in a heavy-based pan.

6   Mix the sauce ingredients, and pour over the eggplants and capsicums. Cover and simmer over a low heat for 1 hour. Add the tomatoes and cook for a further 30 minutes, basting with the sauce occasionally.

serving suggestion
Transfer to a serving dish, drizzle with a little olive oil and the sauce. Serve with Greek-style, plain yoghurt, pickles, fresh herbs** and warmed flatbread.

notes
* See page 18 for instructions on how to make liquid saffron.
**See page 34 for information on suitable types of fresh herbs.

tip

Add the tomatoes in the final 30 minutes, as they require much less cooking than the eggplants and capsicums. With this recipe, it is best to use eggplants that are only slightly larger than capsicums.

kookoo joojeh

CHICKEN FRITTATA

1 Preheat the oven to 180 °C.

2 Heat the oil in a medium-sized, non-stick pan and fry the onion over a medium heat until golden-brown.

3 Add the garlic and chicken and cook for another minute, turning the chicken once. Add the water, salt, pepper and turmeric. Simmer covered, over a low heat for 10 minutes, or until minimal liquid remains. Remove the pan from the heat, allowing it to cool before finely chopping the chicken.

4 Lightly beat the eggs and add the liquid saffron, baking soda and lime juice. Add the chicken and onions and mix well.

5 In a deep-sided frying pan with a removable or heatproof handle, heat the canola oil and 1 tablespoon of the butter until it is sizzling. Once the oil is hot, carefully pour in the mixture and cook uncovered over a medium heat for 15 minutes. Remove from the heat.

6 Pour the remaining melted butter over the surface of the frittata and place it in the oven. Cook for a further 10 minutes. Check to see if it is ready by piercing the centre with a skewer. If it comes out clean, it is cooked.

serving suggestion
Serve warm with a fresh garden salad and yoghurt.

note
*See page 18 for instructions on how to make liquid saffron.

serves 6 | prep 10m | cook 40m

2 tbsp canola oil
2 large brown onions, finely chopped
½ tsp minced garlic
4 boneless chicken thighs
1 cup (250 ml) water
1 tsp salt
½ tsp black pepper
½ tsp turmeric
6 eggs
1 tsp liquid saffron*
1 tsp baking powder
2 tbsp lime juice

for cooking
¼ cup canola oil
2 tbsp butter, melted

Tip
If you don't have a frying pan with a removable or heatproof handle, you can use an ordinary frying pan for the first five stages. At stage 6, place a flat tray, larger than your pan, on top of the kookoo and carefully flip the pan over. Note: Take great care at this stage to avoid serious burns from the hot oil! After this, reheat the pan with the remaining butter, and slide the kookoo back in.

Photo
Vendor selling chickens at the Royan Bazaar, near the Caspian Sea.

Tip

If you don't have a frying pan with a removable or heatproof handle, you can use an ordinary frying pan for the first five stages. At stage 6, place a flat tray, larger than your pan, on top of the kookoo and carefully flip the pan over. Note: Take great care at this stage to avoid serious burns from the hot oil! After this, reheat the pan with the remaining butter, and slide the kookoo back in.

Photo

Vendor selling high quality saffron in Tajrish bazaar, Tehran.

[pronounced / koo-koo bod-em-joon]

kookoo bademjoon

EGGPLANT FRITTATA

serves 6 | **prep** 5m | **cook** 1h 35m

1 large eggplant
2 tbsp canola oil
1 large, brown onion, finely chopped
2 tsp minced garlic
4 eggs
4 tbsp lime juice
1 tsp baking powder
1 tsp salt
½ tsp black pepper
¼ tsp turmeric
1 tbsp liquid saffron*

for cooking
¼ cup canola oil
2 tbsp butter, melted

1   Preheat the oven to 180 °C.

2   Place the eggplant on a gas burner over a high heat, occasionally turning, until the skin is blackened and charred. This step is optional but imparts a beautiful, smoky flavour to the eggplant. If omitting this step, prick the eggplant several times with a fork to prevent it bursting.

3   Wrap the eggplant in aluminium foil, place in an ovenproof dish and bake for 1 hour. Remove from the oven and allow to cool, before removing and discarding the blackened skin and mashing the flesh.

4   Heat the oil in a medium-sized, non-stick frying pan and fry the onion over a medium heat until golden-brown. Add the garlic and cook for a further minute. Remove from the heat and set aside.

5   In a medium-sized mixing bowl, lightly beat the eggs and fold in the eggplant. Add the fried onion and garlic along with the remaining ingredients and mix well.

6   In a deep-sided frying pan with a removable or heatproof handle, heat the canola oil and 1 tbsp of the butter until it is sizzling. Once the oil is hot, carefully pour in the mixture and cook uncovered, over a medium heat for 15 minutes.

7   Remove the pan from the heat and pour the remaining melted butter over the surface of the frittata and place it in the oven. Cook for 10 minutes. Check to see if it is ready by piercing the centre with a skewer. If it comes out clean, it is cooked.

serving suggestion
Cut into eight even-sized pieces. Serve warm or cold with fresh flatbread, Greek-style, plain yoghurt and pickles.

note
*See page 18 for instructions on how to make liquid saffron.

khoresh

Khoresh is the Persian name for the
delicious, melt-in-your-mouth, slow-
cooked stews that feature in the
recipes that follow. It is a rich,
flavoursome stew, with delicately
balanced textures and tastes.

It often has a sweet and sour taste,
which Persians are extremely fond of.
This is due to the addition of
ingredients such as: quince, peach,
plums, unripened grapes, dried limes,
pomegranate purée, verjuice and
tamarind.

Khoresh usually contains some form
of meat, poultry or fish, along with
fruits, vegetables, herbs, nuts and
legumes and is almost always
accompanied by steamed basmati rice.

hearty stews

Ghormeh sabzi would have to be the national dish of Iran. It is, without a doubt, one of the most delicious, all-time favourite stews of Iranian folk.

It has a limey tang that may be a little unusual to the European palette. But, in saying that, after a few tries I have never met anyone who didn't fall in love with it.

[pronounced / ghor-meh sab-zee]

ghormeh sabzi

HERBED LAMB STEW WITH DRIED LIMES

serves
6

prep
45m

cook
2h 15m

2 tbsp canola oil
1.5 kg lamb shoulder or leg, cut into 2 cm x 4 cm chunks
2 large brown onions, finely chopped
1 tsp minced garlic
1 tsp turmeric
1 tsp advieh khorosht*
1 tsp salt
½ tsp black pepper
½ tsp cinnamon
¼ tsp nutmeg
6 cups (1.5 litres) water
6 dried limes**
¼ cup dried fenugreek leaves***
2 tbsp dried lime powder****
½ cup canola oil
2 leeks, green ends only, washed and finely chopped
1 cup spinach leaves, finely chopped
1 cup silverbeet, green leaves only, finely chopped
2 cups fresh, flat-leaf parsley, finely chopped
1 cup fresh chives, finely chopped
1 cup fresh coriander, finely chopped
2 x 420 g tins red kidney beans

1   In a large, heavy-based pan, heat the oil and brown the lamb in small batches, over medium heat for 3—4 minutes. Remove each browned batch with a slotted spoon, then set aside. Browning helps seal in the juices and prevents the meat from falling apart when fully cooked.

2   In the same pan, add a little extra oil if necessary and fry the onion over a medium heat until golden-brown. Add the garlic and cook for another minute.

3   Return the lamb to the pan, sprinkle the turmeric, advieh khoroshte, salt, pepper, cinnamon and nutmeg over the meat and stir briefly. Add the water and bring to the boil.

4   Pierce the dried limes with a fork several times. Add to the pan, along with dried fenugreek leaves and dried lime powder. Cover and simmer gently, over a low heat for 1 hour.

5   Meanwhile, in a large, non-stick pan heat the canola oil and fry the chopped leek, spinach, silverbeet, parsley, chives and coriander over medium heat for 15—20 minutes, stirring frequently. The aroma of the herbs will change, and the oil will turn a greenish colour when squashed with a spoon.

6   Strain and rinse the kidney beans and add to the lamb along with the fried herbs. Cover and continue to simmer gently for a further 1 hour or until the meat is fully cooked and the sauce has reduced slightly.

serving suggestion
Serve with steamed basmati rice and wedges of fresh onion.

notes
*See page 20 for instructions on how to make advieh khorosht (spice blend for stews).
**Dried limes impart a sour, tart taste. They can be left in the food and eaten, or removed prior to serving. They are available from Middle Eastern specialty shops.
***Dried fenugreek leaves have a slightly bitter, curry-like flavour. They are available from Middle Eastern specialty shops.
**** Dried lime powder is made from the crushed, dried black Persian limes. It is optional, but gives the dish an extra tangy, zesty flavour.

tasty tip

For more intense, robust flavours, make your ghormeh sabzi a day or two before you intend to serve and simply reheat as necessary. When reheating ghormeh sabzi or any other khorosht, always reheat over a low to medium flame to avoid the meat falling apart. Khorosht should always be served hot, but not boiling.

degorging

The degorging process makes the eggplant produce a brownish colour sweat, which reduces some of its water content. This helps tenderise the flesh, removes the bitter taste and reduces the amount of oil absorbed during the frying process. To degorge an eggplant, simply peel, slice and sprinkle generously with salt. Allow to stand for 30 minutes before rinsing and thoroughly drying.

khoroshte bademjoon

EGGPLANT & LAMB STEW WITH VERJUICE

1   If using thin eggplants, peel, cut in half lengthwise and set aside. If using the large, common variety, peel and cut lengthwise into 2 cm slices. Cut each slice again in half lengthwise and follow the degorging process on the previous page.

2   In a large, heavy-based pan, heat the oil and brown the lamb in small batches, over a medium heat for 3—4 minutes. Remove each browned batch with a slotted spoon, then set aside. Browning helps seal in the juices and prevents the meat from falling apart when fully cooked.

3   In the same pan, add a little extra oil if necessary and fry the onion over a medium heat until golden-brown. Add the garlic and cook for another minute.

4   Return the lamb to the pan, sprinkle the salt, pepper, cinnamon, nutmeg, turmeric and advieh khorosht over the meat and stir briefly. Add the water, tomato purée, liquid saffron, lime juice and verjuice, and bring to the boil. Cover and simmer gently over a low heat, for 1½ hours.

5   Meanwhile, lightly brush the eggplant with the egg white. Fry both sides over a low to medium heat, until golden-brown. Drain on absorbent paper and continue to cook the remaining eggplant slices. Arrange the fried eggplant over the lamb and simmer for another 30 minutes or until the lamb and eggplant are tender and the sauce has reduced slightly.

serving suggestion
Transfer to a serving dish and serve alongside steamed basmati rice.

notes
*See page 20 for instructions on how to make advieh khorosht (spice blend for stews).
**See page 18 for instructions on how to make liquid saffron.
***Verjuice is the unfermented juice from unripened grapes. It is available from Middle Eastern specialty shops.

serves 6 | prep 30m | cook 2h 15m

9 thin eggplants or
   1 large common variety
2 tbsp canola oil
1.5 kg lamb shoulder or leg,
cut into 2 cm x 4 cm chunks
1 large brown onion, finely
   chopped
1½ tbsp minced garlic
1 tsp salt
½ tsp black pepper
½ tsp cinnamon
¼ tsp nutmeg
1 tsp turmeric
1 tsp advieh khorosht*
6 cups (1.5 litres) water
¼ cup tomato purée
1 tbsp liquid saffron**
1 tbsp lime juice
¼ cup (60 ml) verjuice***
1 egg white
canola oil for frying

ghalieh mahi

CORIANDER & FISH STEW WITH TAMARIND

1   Mix together the fish spicing and use it to lightly coat both sides of the fish.

2   Heat the butter and canola oil in a large, non-stick pan and fry the fish in small batches over a medium heat, until golden-brown and crisp. Remove the cooked fish from the pan, draining off any excess oil on absorbent paper and continue to cook the remainder. Set aside while preparing the coriander sauce.

3   Wipe the pan clean, return to the heat and add the canola oil. Fry the onion over a medium heat until golden-brown. Add the garlic and cook for another minute. Add the salt, pepper, chilli powder, turmeric, curry powder and ground fenugreek seeds. Stir through the onions and continue to cook briefly. Add the chopped coriander, tamarind purée and water and bring to the boil. Lower the heat to minimum, cover and simmer for 30 minutes.

4   Add the fried fish to the coriander sauce and continue to cook for another 10 minutes.

serving suggestion

Serve alongside steamed basmati rice.

hints

*Fenugreek seeds have a slightly bitter, curry-ike flavour. They are hard, oval seeds, about 3 mm in length and should be ground before use.
** Tamarind is a fruit which grows as a pod. It is sweet and sour in taste and is high in vitamin B as well as calcium. It comes as a purée and also in a compressed form. To make purée from compressed tamarind, cover 1/3 cup of the pulp with a 1/3 cup (80 ml) of boiling water. Allow to cool then push the softened pulp through a sieve. Discard the seeds, measure the liquid and use as per the recipe.

serves	prep	cook
6	10m	50m

500 g white fish fillets, cut into
   5 cm lengths

fish spicing
2 tbsp flour
1 tsp salt
½ tsp black pepper
1 tsp turmeric
½ tsp cumin

for frying
4 tbsp butter
1 tbsp canola oil

coriander sauce
2 tbsp canola oil
1 large brown onion, finely chopped
2 tsp minced garlic
½ tsp salt
½ black pepper
½ tsp chilli powder
1 tbsp turmeric
1 tsp curry powder
2 tbsp fenugreek seeds, ground*
3 cups fresh coriander, chopped
¼ cup tamarind purée**
2 cups (500 ml) water

Fesenjoon is a delicious, easy to prepare stew with a distinct sweet and sour taste. It is most commonly made with chicken, but can also be made with lamb meatballs or duck. Some people prefer fesenjoon to be sweet and some sour. The following recipe is a little on the sour side, but can be changed to suit your taste. If you prefer a little sweetness, simply omit the lime juice and add a teaspoon of sugar.

To make fesenjoon with meatballs, simply combine the following ingredients, then form into meatballs the size of walnuts. Add the meatballs in step 5 and cook for 1 hour.

500 g lamb mince
1 large brown onion, grated
1 tsp salt
1/2 tsp black pepper
1/2 tsp turmeric
1/4 cup breadcrumbs
1 egg

[pronounced / fes-n-joon]

fesenjoon

CHICKEN, WALNUT & POMEGRANATE STEW

1   Cut each chicken thigh into four, equal-sized pieces.

2   Heat the oil in a large, heavy-based pan and brown the chicken thighs for 3—4 minutes. Add the chicken seasoning and stir briefly. Remove the thighs from the pan with a slotted spoon and set aside.

3   Return the pan to the heat, add a little more oil if necessary and fry the onion over a medium heat until golden-brown. Add the chopped walnuts, lower the heat to minimum and cook for another 5—6 minutes, stirring constantly to avoid burning the walnuts.

4   Add the tomato and pomegranate purées, chicken stock, salt, pepper, cinnamon and lime juice. Cover and simmer gently for 1 hour.

5   Add the chicken and continue to cook for another 30 minutes.

serving suggestion
Serve alongside steamed basmati rice.

notes
*The walnuts should be chopped finely, but not ground. You still want them to be recognisable as tiny, walnut pieces.
**Pomegranate purée or paste is processed from a sour variety of pomegranate. It gives a beautiful, rich flavour and colour to dishes and is famous for its pairing with walnuts.

serves	prep	cook
6	20m	1h 40m

1.5 kg boneless chicken thighs, skin removed
2 tsp canola oil
1 tsp chicken seasoning
1 large brown onion, finely chopped
2 cups walnuts, finely chopped*
3 tbsp tomato purée
1/2 cup pomegranate purée**
4 cups (1 litre) chicken stock
1 tsp salt
1/2 tsp black pepper
1/2 tsp cinnamon
1 tbsp lime juice

Khoroshte aloo is a flavoursome, warming, easy to make stew with a slightly sweet and sour taste.

In Iran they use a yellow variety of prune. As this may be difficult to find, the common black prune works just as well.

khoroshte aloo

CHICKEN & PRUNE STEW WITH SAFFRON

serves 6

prep 10m

cook 1h 15m

2 tbsp canola oil
6 chicken drumsticks, or mixed pieces
1 cup pitted prunes
1 large brown onion, finely sliced
1 tbsp minced garlic
1 tsp turmeric
1 tsp salt
½ tsp black pepper
¼ tsp cinnamon
3 tsp liquid saffron*
2 cups (500 ml) water
2 tbsp tomato purée

1   Preheat the oven to 190 °C.

2   In a large, non-stick pan heat the oil and fry the chicken over a medium heat until golden-brown. Remove from the pan, with a slotted spoon and transfer to a baking dish. Add the prunes and set aside.

3   Return the pan to the heat, add a little extra oil if necessary and fry the onion over a medium heat until golden-brown. Add the garlic and cook for another minute.

4   Sprinkle the turmeric, salt, pepper and cinnamon over the onions and stir briefly.

5   Add the liquid saffron, water and tomato purée and bring to the boil. Deglaze the pan by gently scraping any browned bits from the bottom with a wooden spoon.

6   Remove the pan from the heat and pour the sauce over the chicken and prunes. Cover with aluminium foil and bake for 45 minutes. After 45 minutes, remove the foil and continue to cook for another 15 minutes.

serving suggestion
Delicious served with steamed basmati rice or baked jacket potatoes and steamed greens.

note
*See page 18 for instructions on how to make liquid saffron.

quick tip

Thin potato straws
or Twisties® can also
be used as a garnish
to save time.

[pronounced / ghay-meh]

gheimeh

LAMB & SPLIT PEA STEW WITH POTATO-STRAW GARNISH

1 In a large, heavy-based pan, heat the oil and brown the lamb in small batches, over a medium heat for 3—4 minutes. Remove each browned batch with a slotted spoon, then set aside. Browning helps seal in the juices and prevents the meat from falling apart when fully cooked.

2 In the same pan, add a little extra oil if necessary and fry the onion over a medium heat until golden-brown. Add the garlic and cook for another minute.

3 Return the lamb to the pan. Sprinkle the salt, pepper, cinnamon, advieh khorosht and turmeric over the lamb and stir briefly.

4 Peirce the dried limes several times with a fork and add to the lamb along with the water, tomato purée and liquid saffron and bring to the boil. Reduce the heat to minimum, cover and simmer for 1½ hours.

5 Meanwhile, in a small saucepan cook the split peas in 3 cups (750 ml) of boiling, salted water for 20 minutes. Strain, rinse under cool water and set aside. The split peas should be tender but not mushy.

6 Add the split peas to the lamb and simmer gently over a low heat for another 20 minutes. Transfer to a serving dish, cover with aluminium foil and keep warm while preparing the potato-straw garnish.

7 To prepare the potato-straw garnish, pat dry the potato matchsticks to remove any excess starch and gently heat the canola oil. Test if the oil is hot enough by placing one or two potato matchsticks into the hot oil. If the oil is hot enough, bubbles will immediately form around the potato matchstick. Fry the potato matchsticks in small batches, for 2—3 minutes or until they are crisp and golden-brown. Remove the cooked potato matchsticks with a slotted spoon, drain on absorbent paper and continue cooking the remainder.

serving suggestion

Garnish with stew with potato straws and serve immediately. Serve alongside steamed basmati rice.

notes

*Dried limes are available from Middle Eastern speciality shops. They impart a delicious sour, tart taste to dishes. If you can't source them, you can substitute with 1—2 tsp of lime juice.
**See page 20 for instructions on how to make advieh khorosht (spice blend for stews).
***See page 18 for instructions on how to make liquid saffron.

serves 6 | prep 20m | cook 2h

2 tbsp canola oil
1 kg stewing lamb, cut into 1½ cm cubes
2 large brown onions, finely chopped
1 tsp minced garlic
1 tsp salt
½ tsp black pepper
¼ tsp cinnamon
1 tsp advieh khorosht**
1 tbsp turmeric
4 dried limes*
6 cups (1.5 litres) water
3 tbsp tomato purée
2 tsp liquid saffron***
1½ cup yellow split peas

potato-straw garnish
¼ cup canola oil
2 large potatoes, peeled and sliced into matchsticks

Quince are an ancient, autumn fruit which grow on small trees, quite similar to apples. They are not at all well known and are usually quite hard to find.

The fruit, irregular in shape, has a yellow, fuzzy skin with whitish inner flesh. It is astringent, hard and almost inedible when raw, but once cooked is a totally different story.

Once cooked, the hard, inedible flesh becomes soft and changes into a beautiful, reddish-pink colour with an amazing perfume.

[pronounced / kho-roasht-eh beh]

khoroshte beh

TANGY QUINCE & LAMB STEW

serves 6   **prep** 20m   **cook** 2h 10m

4 tbsp canola oil
2 large brown onions, finely chopped
4 tbsp lemon juice
750 g stewing lamb, cut into 2½ cm cubes
6 cups (1.5 litres) water
4 tbsp tomato purée
1 tsp salt
1 tsp turmeric
½ tsp black pepper
½ tsp cinnamon
1 tsp liquid saffron*
4 medium quince

1 Heat 2 tablespoons of the oil in a large, heavy-based pan and fry the onion over a medium heat until golden-brown. With a slotted spoon, remove the onion from the pan, place in a small bowl, mix with the lemon juice and set aside.

2 Return the pan to the heat and add the lamb in small batches. Brown the lamb, over a medium heat for 3—4 minutes. Remove each browned batch with a slotted spoon and set aside. Browning helps seal in the juices and prevents the meat from falling apart when fully cooked.

3 Return the browned lamb and onion to the pan. Add the water, tomato purée, spices and liquid saffron. Cover and simmer over a low heat for 1½ hours. The meat should be almost cooked, but not falling apart.

4 Meanwhile, wash and core the quince but do not peel. It is very important to remove the core as it is too hard to eat, even after cooking. Slice the quince into eight, evenly sized wedges so they end up a similar size to apples in apple pie.

5 Heat the remaining oil in a medium, non-stick pan and fry the quince over a low to medium heat until golden-brown. Remove from the pan, draining off any excess oil on absorbent paper.

6 Add the quince to the pan and simmer, covered for a further 30 minutes or until the meat and quince are tender.

serving suggestion
Serve with steamed basmati rice.

note
*See page 18 for instructions on how to make liquid saffron.

substitution

Green cooking apples also work
well if quince are out of season.
Simply add the apple in the last
15 minutes of cooking as they have
a tendency to turn to mush if
overcooked.

khoroshte hooloo

SWEET & SOUR PEACH & CHICKEN STEW

1   Wash the peaches and cut in half. Remove and discard the stone and slice into eight, evenly sized wedges. They should end up a similar size to the apples in apple pie.

2   Heat the oil in a large, heavy-based pan and fry the peaches in small batches, until golden-brown. Remove the cooked peaches from the pan and draining off any excess oil on absorbent paper. Continue cooking the remainder and set aside.

3   Return the pan to the heat, add the onion and fry over a medium heat until golden-brown. Add the garlic and cook for another minute.

4   Add the chicken thighs to the pan and brown lightly to seal in the juices. Add the salt, pepper, paprika and chicken seasoning and briefly stir it through the chicken.

5   Arrange the peach wedges on top of the chicken and onion.

6   Mix together the sauce ingredients and pour over the chicken and peaches. Cover and simmer over a low heat, for 30 minutes.

serving suggestion
Serve with steamed basmati rice.

note
*See page 18 for instructions on how to make liquid saffron.

serves 6 | **prep** 10m | **cook** 40m

4 large peaches, under-ripe
3 tbsp canola oil
1 large brown onion, finely sliced
1 tsp minced garlic
1 kg boneless chicken thighs, cut into four equal-sized pieces
1 tsp salt
½ tsp black pepper
¼ tsp paprika
1 tsp chicken seasoning

sauce
2 cups (500 ml) water
2 tbsp lime juice
¼ cup tomato purée
1 tsp liquid saffron*

Fresh celery is an excellent source of non-soluble fibre, vitamin K and has anti-inflammatory properties.

The leaves are rich in antioxidants, vitamin A, potassium and beta-carotene and can be eaten fresh in salads or cooked.

Always consume celery within 5 days, to retain optimum freshness. To preserve the maximum nutrients possible, always chop celery just before eating or cooking.

[pronounced / kho-roasht-eh ka-rafs]

khoroshte karafs

HERBED LAMB STEW WITH CELERY & DRIED LIMES

serves 6 | **prep** 20m | **cook** 2h

4 tbsp canola oil
1 kg stewing lamb, cut into
    1.5 cm cubes
2 large brown onions, finely
    chopped
1 tbsp minced garlic
1 tsp salt
½ tsp black pepper
½ tsp cinnamon
1 tsp turmeric
2 tbsp dried mint
¼ tsp nutmeg
6 cups (1.5 litres) water
2 tsp liquid saffron*
4 dried limes
1 bunch celery
2 cups fresh flat-leaf parsley,
    finely chopped

1   In a large, heavy-based pan, heat 2 tablespoons of the oil and brown the lamb in small batches, over a medium heat for 3—4 minutes. Remove each browned batch with a slotted spoon, then set aside. Browning helps seal in the juices and prevents the meat from falling apart when fully cooked.

2   In the same pan, add a little extra oil if necessary and fry the onion over a medium heat until golden-brown. Add the garlic and cook for another minute.

3   Sprinkle the spices over the lamb and stir briefly. Add the water and liquid saffron and bring to the boil.

4   Pierce the dried limes with a fork several times and add to the pan. Cover and simmer over a low heat for 30 minutes.

5   Meanwhile, wash and dry the celery and cut into 3 cm lengths.

6   Heat the remaining oil in a large, deep-sided pan and fry the celery over a medium heat for 10 minutes. Stir frequently to prevent the celery from burning. Add the parsley and continue to cook for a further 5 minutes.

7   Add the celery and parsley to the lamb and simmer over a low heat for a further 1.5 hours or until the meat is fully cooked.

serving suggestion
Serve with steamed basmati rice.

note
*See page 18 for instructions on how to make liquid saffron.

tasty tip

For more intense flavours, make khoroshte karafs the day before you intend to serve and simply reheat as necessary. When reheating any khorosht, always reheat over a low to medium flame, to avoid the meat falling apart. Khorosht should always be served hot, but not boiling.

quick tip

Frozen okra can also be used to speed things up, or if fresh is unavailable. Simply defrost and add to the stew 10 minutes before serving.

[pronounced / kho-roasht-eh baa-mee-eh]

khoroshte bamieh

CHICKEN, TOMATO & OKRA STEW

1   Wash and pat dry the okra and trim any hard stem tops down to 1 cm in length. Heat the oil in a large, heavy-based pan, and fry the okra over a medium heat for 5 minutes, stirring frequently. Remove the okra from the pan, draining off any excess oil on absorbent paper and set aside.

2   Return the pan to the heat and fry the onion over a medium heat until golden-brown. Add the garlic and cook for another minute.

3   Add the chicken and brown lightly to seal in the juices. Add the salt, pepper and turmeric and stir through the chicken.

4   Mix together the lime juice, tomato purée, chicken stock, tomato juice and liquid saffron, pour over the chicken and bring to the boil. Reduce the heat to minimum, cover and simmer gently for 45 minutes, stirring occasionally.

5   Add the okra to the chicken, cover and simmer over a low heat for another 20 minutes.

serving suggestion
Serve with steamed basmati rice.

note
*See page 18 for instructions on how to make liquid saffron.

serves 6

prep 20m

cook 1h 15m

500 g fresh okra
4 tbsp canola oil
1 large brown onion, finely chopped
2 tsp minced garlic
1 kg mixed chicken pieces
1 tsp salt
½ tsp black pepper
1 tbsp turmeric
2 tbsp lime juice
2 tbsp tomato purée
1 cup (250 ml) chicken stock
1 cup (250 ml) tomato juice
2 tsp liquid saffron*

berenj

Berenj is the Persian word for rice.
The aim in cooking Persian rice is to
make a beautiful, fluffy rice, where
each grain separates. This is achieved
through soaking, parboiling, straining
and finally steaming.

Aged basmati is well suited to Persian
cooking due to its long grains. It is
available in most supermarkets.
However, you need to choose
a high-grade basmati to get the best
results. Don't worry if the rice looks a
little yellow; it will turn white when
cooked.

Persian rice dishes often include
various meats, legumes,
herbs, nuts, fruit and spices mixed
together to create a delicious, colourful
and fragrant rice.

rice dishes

[pronounced / chel-ow]

chelo

STEAMED BASMATI RICE

serves 6 | **prep** 5m | **soak** 1h | **cook** 1h

3 cups basmati rice
1 tbsp salt

tah dig (golden crust)
1 large pita bread, or
  1 large potato, cut into ½ cm slices

for cooking
¼ cup canola oil
¼ tsp turmeric
2 tbsp butter, melted
2 tsp liquid saffron*
¼ cup (60 ml) water

garnish
2 tsp liquid saffron*

Rice paddies in Iran are
concentrated in the Caspian
Sea region, mainly in the
provinces of Gilan and
Mazandaran.

This is due to the
abundant, annual rainfall
in the lowlands of these
regions and a network of
rivers and streams.

Although favourable, the
conditions are less than
prefect due to the cold
winter months limiting the
growing season to one crop
per year.

1   Rinse the rice thoroughly under running water, until the water runs clear. Transfer the rice into a large, heavy-based pan. Add the salt and enough water to cover the rice by about 10 cm. Soak for 1 hour. Note: Rinsing removes some of the starch from the rice, making it less susceptible to sticking together. The salt preserves the shape and adds flavour.

2   Place the pan with presoaked rice onto the stove top, adding a little extra water if necessary and bring it to the boil. Stir once, to separate the grains. Once boiling, continue to cook until the rice is 'al dente'. This process should take about 5—7 minutes, once the water has boiled. To test if the rice is ready for the next step, carefully remove a grain or two and bite through to the centre. The rice should be firm in the centre and soft on the outside. Strain the rice and rinse thoroughly under cool water. This prevents the rice from cooking any further, while you prepare the tah dig.

3   Return the empty pan to the stove top and add the canola oil. Once it is sizzling, add the turmeric and swirl gently to distribute and colour the oil. Carefully place the bread or potatoes on the bottom of the pan and spoon in the parboiled rice. Form the rice into a mound and poke a few holes deep into the rice so the steam can circulate.

4   Mix the melted butter, liquid saffron and water together and pour some of it over the rice. Cover the pan with a clean tea towel and place the lid on the pan. Tie the ends of the tea towel together on top of the lid to prevent them from catching fire. After 30 seconds, turn the heat down to minimum and steam the rice for 45 minutes.

5   After 45 minutes, carefully remove the lid and check to see if the rice is fully cooked. If necessary, add a little more of the prepared saffron, butter and water mix. Place the lid back on and continue to cook for another 15 minutes.

6   To check if the tah dig is ready, wet your finger and quickly tap the side of the pan, approximately 3 cm from the base. If you see a sizzle and hear a small hiss, the tah dig is ready.

serving suggestion
Spoon the rice onto a large flat tray, reserving 3—4 tablespoons of rice for garnish. Mix together the reserved rice with the liquid saffron and spoon over the top of the rice. Gently scrape the tah dig from the bottom of the pan and serve on a separate plate. Tip: Leaving the tah dig in the pan for a few minutes to cool slightly helps to release it from the pan. Serve with your choice of kebab or khoresh.

note
*See page 18 for instructions on how to make liquid saffron.

techniques & tips (rice making)

RIGHT

rinse & repeat

It is very important to wash and rinse the rice thoroughly until the water runs clear. This process helps remove excess starch from the rice to ensure the finished rice will be fluffy and won't stick together.

BELOW

testing

To check if the rice is ready for straining, carefully remove a few grains and bite through to the centre. When ready, the rice will be still slightly firm in the centre but soft on the outside. If you can see a dark spot in the centre, it needs a little more cooking.

aged or fresh

Aged basmati is perfect for cooking Persian rice dishes. During the ageing process, the rice dries out completely and, therefore, can absorb more water during the cooking process. This results in a beautiful, long-grained rice, where each grain is non-sticky and separates.

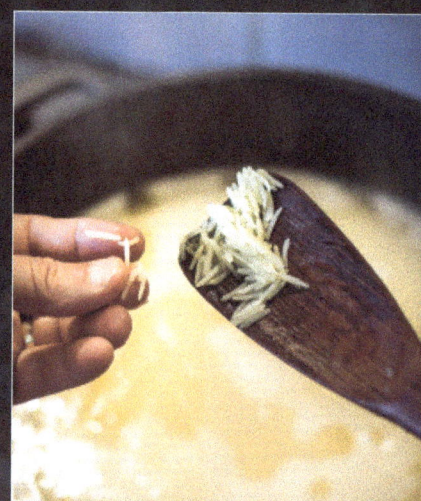

ABOVE

straining

It is important to strain and rinse the rice under cool water, to stop the cooking process immediately. If you don't do this, the rice will continue to cook while you prepare the tah dig, and will become sticky.

LEFT

steaming

The tea towel tied around the lid of the pan provides a tight, snug fit, which seals in the moisture. It also catches the steam that turns to water. Without this, the water would drip on the rice below, ruining it.

tah dig (the golden crust)

RIGHT

serving tip

The tah dig should be served on a separate plate to your rice, and cut into small, golden shards. This is, unless it's a rice that is flipped over, rather than spooned out. If using flatbread, you can also cut it up, before placing in the pan.

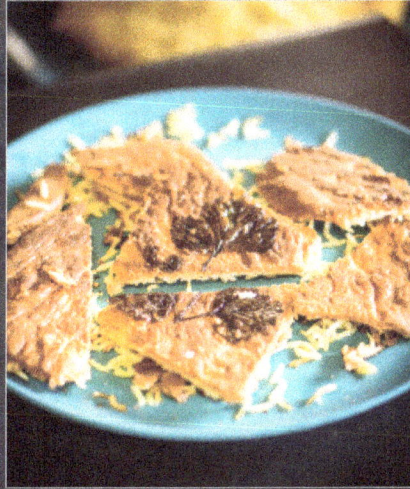

BELOW

types of tah dig

Tah dig can be made from many ingredients. These include the rice itself, rice mixed with yoghurt and egg, noodles, flatbread, potato, cabbage and even lettuce.

releasing tip

Remove the pan with the cooked rice and tah dig from the heat. Leave it covered and untouched for a few minutes, to cool slightly. This helps the tah dig release from the pan.

ABOVE

reheating tip

If you want to prepare your rice with tah dig before guests arrive, but don't want it to go soft, cook your rice with tah dig as normal. Once ready, remove the pan from the heat, and set aside. When required, reheat, over a low heat, for 20 minutes.

LEFT

checking

To check if the tah dig is ready, wet your finger and quickly tap the side of the pan, approximately 3 cm from the base. If you see a sizzle and hear a small hiss, then the tah dig is ready.

tah chin

SAFFRON RICE PILAF WITH CHICKEN & YOGHURT

1   In a medium-sized frying pan, heat the olive oil and fry the onion over a medium heat until golden-brown. Add the garlic and cook for another minute. Sprinkle the salt, pepper and turmeric over the onions and stir through. Place the chicken on top of the onions and add the water. Cover and simmer over a low to medium heat for 10 minutes or until minimal liquid remains. Set aside to cool, then tear the chicken into strips.

2   Meanwhile, prepare the barberries. Heat the olive oil in a small frying pan, add the barberries and fry over a low to medium heat for 1 minute. Add the liquid saffron and lime juice and continue cooking for 1–2 minutes. It is very important to stir constantly to prevent the barberries from burning. Remove from the heat and set aside.

3   In an airtight container with a lid, mix the marinade ingredients together. Add the chicken and onion and refrigerate for 2 hours.

4   Rinse the rice thoroughly under running water, until the water runs clear. Transfer the rice into a large, heavy-based pan. Add the salt, turmeric and enough water to cover the rice by about 10 cm. Soak for 1 hour. Note: Rinsing removes some of the starch from the rice, making it less susceptible to sticking together. The salt preserves the shape and adds flavour.

notes
*See page 18 for instructions on how to make liquid saffron.
**Barberries are a sour, dried fruit available from Middle Eastern specialty shops.

continued over page...

Tah chin is often made for special occasions and often features in weddings. The way the tah chin is cooked develops a golden, crispy, outer crust and a soft, fragrant inner.

It is a beautifully perfumed dish and the barberries complement the chicken perfectly.

serves 6 | **prep** 10m | **soak** 1h | **cook** 2h

+ 2h marinating

chicken
2 tbsp olive oil
1 large brown onion, finely sliced
1 tsp minced garlic
1 tsp salt
½ tsp black pepper
1 tbsp turmeric
500g boneless chicken thighs
¼ cup (60 ml) water

barberries
1 tbsp olive oil
1 cup barberries**
1 tbsp liquid saffron*
1 tbsp lime juice

marinade
1 cup Greek-style, plain yoghurt
3 tbsp liquid saffron*
1 tsp salt
½ tsp black pepper
2 tbsp orange zest
¼ cup (60 ml) rosewater

rice
3 cups basmati rice
1 tbsp salt
½ tsp turmeric

tah chin cont...

SAFFRON RICE PILAF WITH CHICKEN & YOGHURT

serves **6** prep **10m** soak **1h** cook **2h**

+ 2h marinating

tah dig (golden crust)
2 eggs, lightly beaten
2 tbsp liquid saffron*
2 tbsp Greek-style, plain yoghurt

for cooking
¼ cup canola oil
2 tbsp butter, melted

5   Place the pan with presoaked rice onto the stove top, adding a little extra water if necessary and bring it to the boil. Stir once, to separate the grains. Once boiling, continue to cook until the rice is 'al dente'. This process should take about 5—7 minutes, once the water has boiled. To test if the rice is ready for the next step, carefully remove a grain or two and bite through to the centre. The rice should be firm in the centre and soft on the outside. Strain the rice and rinse thoroughly under cool water. This prevents the rice from cooking any further, while you prepare the tah dig.

6   Squeeze any excess marinade from the chicken and reserve.

7   Prepare the tah dig by mixing together 1 cup of the parboiled rice with the reserved marinade, beaten eggs, liquid saffron and yoghurt.

8   Return the empty pan to the stove top and add the canola oil. Once the oil is sizzling, line the bottom of the pan with the prepared tah dig mixture. Spoon half the parboiled rice on top of the tah dig. Add the chicken and barberries to create the middle layer and finally spoon in the remaining rice. Use a wooden spoon to pack the rice down. Pour the melted butter over the rice. Cover the pan with a clean tea towel and place the lid on the pan. Tie the ends of the tea towel together on top of the lid to prevent them from catching fire. After 30 seconds, turn the heat down to the minimum and steam the rice for 1½ hours.

9   To check if the tah dig is ready, wet your finger and quickly tap the side of the pan, approximately 3 cm from the base. If you see a sizzle and hear a small hiss, the tah dig is ready.

serving suggestion
To serve, remove the pan from the heat and allow to cool for 5 minutes, without removing the lid. After 5 minutes, carefully remove the lid and place a large flat, round tray over the pan. Hold firmly with both hands and flip the rice upside down onto the tray. Slice like a cake in to 6 evenly sized portions.

note
*See page 18 for instructions on how to make liquid saffron.

baghali polo

DILL & BROAD BEAN RICE WITH LAMB SHANKS

1   Rinse the rice thoroughly under running water, until the water runs clear. Transfer the rice into a large, heavy-based pan. Add the salt, turmeric and enough water to cover the rice by about 10 cm. Soak for 1 hour. Note: Rinsing removes some of the starch from the rice, making it less susceptible to sticking together. The salt preserves the shape and adds flavour.

2   Meanwhile in a large, heavy-based frying pan, heat the olive oil and fry the onion over a medium heat until golden-brown. Add the garlic and cook for another minute.

3   Add the lamb shanks and brown all over. Sprinkle the salt, pepper, cinnamon, turmeric and advieh khorosht over the lamb shanks and stir through. Add the water, dill, liquid saffron and lime juice. Cover and simmer over a low heat for 3 hours, or until the lamb shanks are tender.

4   Place the frozen broad beans in hot water for 5 minutes. Strain off the water, remove the outer shell and set aside.

5   Place the pan with presoaked rice onto the stove top, adding a little extra water if necessary and bring it to the boil. Stir once, to separate the grains. Once boiling, continue to cook until the rice is 'al dente'. This process should take about 5—7 minutes, once the water has boiled. To test if the rice is ready for the next step, carefully remove a grain or two and bite through to the centre. The rice should be firm in the centre and soft on the outside. Strain the rice and rinse thoroughly under cool water. Gently mix together with the shelled broad beans and dill.

6   Return the empty pan to the stove top and add the canola oil. Once it is sizzling, add the turmeric and swirl gently to distribute and colour the oil. Note: It is important to use a medium to large gas ring over the lowest heat setting. This ensures the heat is distributed evenly and does not burn the rice in one spot. Carefully place the potato slices on the bottom of the pan and spoon in the parboiled, mixed rice. Form the rice into a mound and poke a few holes deep into the rice so the steam can circulate.

7   Mix the melted butter, liquid saffron and water together and pour some of it over the rice. Cover the pan with a clean tea towel and place the lid on the pan. Tie the ends of the tea towel together on top of the lid to prevent them from catching fire. After 30 seconds, turn the heat down to minimum and steam the rice for 1 hour.

8   After 1 hour, carefully remove the lid and check if the rice is fully cooked. If necessary, add a little more of the prepared saffron, butter and water mix. Place the lid back on and continue to cook for another 15 minutes.

9   To check if the tah dig is ready, wet your finger and quickly tap the side of the pan, approximately 3 cm from the base. If you see a sizzle and hear a small hiss, then the tah dig is ready.

serving suggestion
Spoon the rice onto a large flat tray. Reserve 3—4 tablespoons of the rice for garnish. Mix the reserved rice with liquid saffron and spoon over the top of the rice. Gently scrape the tah dig from the bottom of the pan and serve on a separate plate. Serve with the prepared lamb shanks, Greek-style, plain yoghurt and pickled garlic.

serves	prep	soak	cook
6	20m	1h	3h

dill and broad bean rice
3 cups basmati rice
1 tbsp salt
pinch of turmeric
500 g broad beans, frozen
¼ cup dried dill

lamb shanks
2 tbsp olive oil
1 large brown onion, finely chopped
1 tsp minced garlic
6 lamb shanks
1 tsp salt
½ tsp black pepper
½ tsp cinnamon
1 tsp turmeric
1 tsp advieh khorosht*
6 cups (1.5 litres) water
2 tbsp dried dill
2 tsp liquid saffron**
2 tbsp lime juice

tah dig (golden crust)
1 large potato, cut into ½ cm slices

for cooking
¼ cup canola oil
¼ tsp turmeric
2 tbsp butter, melted
2 tsp liquid saffron**
¼ cup (60 ml) water

garnish
2 tsp liquid saffron**

notes
*See page 20 for Persian spice blend for stews (advieh khorosht).
**See page 18 for instructions on how to make liquid saffron.

sabzi polo ba mahi (part 1)

HERBED RICE WITH FISH

serves 6
prep 10m
soak 1h
cook 1h 20m

3 cups basmati rice
1 tbsp salt
pinch of turmeric
½ cup fresh dill, or 3 tbsp dried dill
½ cup fresh coriander
1 cup fresh, flat-leaf parsley
½ cup fresh chives
1 tsp minced garlic
1 tsp dried fenugreek seeds,
    ground**
½ tsp black pepper
½ tsp cinnamon
½ tsp cumin

tah dig (golden crust)
1 large pita bread, or
    1 large potato, cut into ½ cm slices

for cooking
¼ cup canola oil
¼ tsp turmeric
2 tbsp butter, melted
2 tsp liquid saffron*
¼ cup (60 ml) water

to serve
2 tbsp liquid saffron*

1   Rinse the rice thoroughly under running water, until the water runs clear. Transfer the rice into a large, heavy-based pan. Add the salt, turmeric and enough water to cover the rice by about 10 cm. Soak for 1 hour. Note: Rinsing removes some of the starch from the rice, making it less susceptible to sticking together. The salt preserves the shape and adds flavour.

2   Wash and finely chop the fresh dill, coriander, parsley and chives. Mix the herbs together with the garlic, ground fenugreek seeds, pepper, cinnamon and cumin. Set aside.

3   Place the pan with presoaked rice onto the stove top, adding a little extra water if necessary and bring it to the boil. Stir once, to separate the grains. Once boiling, continue to cook until the rice is 'al dente'. This process should take about 5–7 minutes, once the water has boiled. To test if the rice is ready for the next step, carefully remove a grain or two and bite through to the centre. The rice should be firm in the centre and soft on the outside. Strain the rice and rinse thoroughly under cool water. This prevents the rice from cooking any further, while you prepare the tah dig.

4   Gently mix the parboiled rice together with the mixed herbs and garlic.

5   Return the empty pan to the stove top and add the canola oil. Once it is sizzling, add the turmeric and swirl gently to distribute and colour the oil. Note: It is important to use a medium to large gas ring over the lowest heat setting. This ensures the heat is distributed evenly and does not burn the rice in one spot. Carefully place the bread or potatoes on the bottom of the pan and spoon in the mixed parboiled rice. Form the rice into a mound and poke a few holes deep into the rice so the steam can circulate.

6   Mix the melted butter, liquid saffron and water together and pour some of it over the rice. Cover the pan with a clean tea towel and place the lid on the pan. Tie the ends of the tea towel together on top of the lid to prevent them from catching fire. After 30 seconds, turn the heat down to minimum and steam the rice for 1 hour.

7   Meanwhile, prepare and cook mahi sefid (fried white fish—see page 143).

serving suggestion
Spoon the rice onto a large flat tray, reserving 6 tablespoons of rice for garnish. Mix together the reserved rice with the liquid saffron and spoon over the top of the rice. Gently scrape the tah dig from the bottom of the pan and serve on a separate plate. Tip: Leaving the tah dig in the pan for a few minutes to cool slightly helps to release it from the pan. Serve with the fried white fish, lime wedges and pickled garlic.

notes
*See page 18 for instructions on how to make liquid saffron.
**Fenugreek seeds have a slightly bitter, curry-like flavour. They are hard, oval seeds, about 3 mm in length and should be ground before use.

continued over page...

sabzi polo ba mahi (part 2)

FRIED WHITE FISH

1   In a medium-sized bowl, mix the flour together with the lemon pepper, salt, pepper and turmeric.

2   In a separate bowl, whisk the eggs together with the milk, garlic, salt and liquid saffron.

3   Dredge each fish fillet in the flour mixture and then into the egg mixture. Allow any excess to drop off and then, once again, dredge the fillet into the flour.

4   Heat the canola oil and fry the fish fillets over a medium heat, until lightly golden. This should take approximately 2 minutes per side, depending on the thickness of the fish. Allow the oil to come back to temperature before frying the next batch and take care not to overcook. Once cooked, place the fish on paper towel to soak up any excess oil, cover with aluminium foil and keep warm.

note
*See page 18 for instructions on how to make liquid saffron.

traditional
Mahi sefid together with sabzi polo are always served as part of the Persian Noruz celebrations.

serves 6 | prep 10m | cook 10m

6 barramundi fillets, or
    any white fish you prefer

flour dredge
1 cup self-raising flour
3 tbsp lemon pepper
1 tsp salt
½ tsp black pepper
1 tsp turmeric

egg wash
3 eggs
¼ cup (60 ml) milk
1 tsp minced garlic
1 tsp salt
2 tbsp liquid saffron*

for frying
½ cup canola oil

javaher polo

JEWELLED RICE

serves	prep	soak	cook
6	30m	1h	2h

rice
3 cups basmati rice
1 tbsp salt
pinch of turmeric

rubies
1 cup barberries *
2 tbsp olive oil
2 large brown onions,
    finely chopped
2 tbsp butter
2 tbsp lime juice
2 tsp liquid saffron**
2 tbsp water

ambers
3 oranges
2 tbsp butter
2 tbsp canola oil
3 large carrots, peeled
    and cut into matchsticks
2 tbsp honey
½ tsp cinnamon
½ tsp cardamom
½ tsp cumin
1 tsp advieh polo***
1 cup (250 ml) water
2 tbsp orange blossom water

jades, pearls & garnets
1 tbsp butter
½ cup almond slices
½ cup pistachio kernels
½ cup sultanas
2 tbsp dried rose petals

1   Rinse the rice thoroughly under running water, until the water runs clear. Transfer the rice into a large, heavy-based pan. Add the salt, turmeric and enough water to cover the rice by about 10 cm. Soak for 1 hour. Note: Rinsing removes some of the starch from the rice, making it less susceptible to sticking together. The salt preserves the shape and adds flavour.

2   Wash, strain and sort through the barberries to remove any stems or small stones.

3   In a medium-sized, non-stick pan, heat the olive oil and fry the onion over a medium heat until golden-brown. Add the butter and barberries and cook for another minute, constantly stirring as they burn easily. Add the lime juice, liquid saffron and water and simmer over a low heat for 2 minutes. Remove from the heat and set aside.

4   Remove the skin from the oranges using a vegetable peeler and cut it into matchsticks. Try not to remove too much of the white, bitter pith. Place the orange skin slivers in a small pan of boiling water and simmer for 5 minutes before straining the water.

5   In a medium-sized saucepan, melt the butter and canola oil. Add the carrots, oranges, honey, cinnamon, cardamom, cumin and advieh polo. Stir briefly before adding the water and orange blossom water. Simmer, uncovered over a medium heat for 10 minutes. Strain and reserve the syrup for later.

6   Melt the butter and fry the almonds and pistachios over a low heat for 2 minutes, stirring constantly. Stir in the sultanas and dried rose petals, remove from the heat and set aside.

notes
*Barberries are a sour, dried fruit available from Middle Eastern specialty shops.
**See page 18 for instructions on how to make liquid saffron.
***See page 20 for instructions on how to make advieh polo (spice blend for rice).

continued over page...

rinse & soak

cut into matchsticks

cut orange peel

caramelise 10 minutes

fry onion & barberries

fry 30 seconds

mix together

pour syrup over

prepare tah dig

javaher polo cont...

JEWELLED RICE

8 Place the pan with presoaked rice onto the stove top, adding a little extra water if necessary and bring it to the boil. Stir once, to separate the grains. Once boiling, continue to cook until the rice is 'al dente'. This process should take about 5—7 minutes, once the water has boiled. To test if the rice is ready for the next step, carefully remove a grain or two and bite through to the centre. The rice should be firm in the centre and soft on the outside. Strain the rice and rinse thoroughly under cool water.

9 Gently mix the prepared barberries, orange slivers, carrots and nuts together with the rice.

10 Prepare the tah dig by mixing 6 heaped tablespoons of the cooked rice together with the yoghurt, beaten egg and liquid saffron.

11 Return the empty pan to the stove top and add the canola oil. Once it is sizzling, carefully spread the tah dig mixture over the bottom of the pan. Spoon in the parboiled mixed rice. Form the rice into a mound and poke a few holes deep into the rice so the steam can circulate. Drizzle some of the caramelised liquid over the rice. Cover the pan with a clean tea towel and place the lid on the pan. Tie the ends of the tea towel together on top of the lid to prevent them from catching fire. After 30 seconds, turn the heat down to minimum and steam the rice for 1 hour 15 minutes.

12 After 1 hour 15 minutes, carefully remove the lid and check if the rice is fully cooked. If necessary, add a little more of the caramelised liquid. Place the lid back on and continue to cook for another 15 minutes.

13 To check if the tah dig is ready, wet your finger and quickly tap the side of the pan, approximately 3 cm from the base. If you see a sizzle and hear a small hiss, then the tah dig is ready.

serving suggestion
Spoon the rice onto a large flat tray and form into a mound. Serve the tah dig (golden crust) broken into pieces on a separate plate. Javaher polo is delicious served with jujeh kebab (saffron & lime chicken wings — see page 192).

note
*See page 18 for instructions on how to make liquid saffron.

serves	prep	soak	cook
6	30m	1h	2h

tah dig (golden crust)
2 tbsp Greek style, plain yoghurt
1 egg, beaten
2 tbsp liquid saffron*

for cooking
¼ cup canola oil

lubia polo

RICE WITH GREEN BEANS

1   Rinse the rice thoroughly under running water, until the water runs clear. Transfer the rice into a large, heavy-based pan. Add the salt, turmeric and enough water to cover the rice by about 10 cm. Soak for 1 hour. Note: Rinsing removes some of the starch from the rice, making it less susceptible to sticking together. The salt preserves the shape and adds flavour.

2   Top and tail the green beans and cut into 2 cm lengths.

3   Heat the olive oil in a large, non-stick pan and fry the onion over a medium heat until golden-brown. Add the garlic and green beans and cook for another 10 minutes, frequently stirring. Remove the onion and beans from the pan and set aside.

4   Reheat the pan, add the lamb mince and fry over a medium heat, frequently stirring to break up any lumps. Add the spices and stir briefly. Pierce the dried limes several times with a fork. Add to the pan along with the tomato purée, tomatoes and water. Stir to combine. Return the onion and green beans to the pan. Cover and simmer over a low heat, for 30 minutes or until almost no water remains. Remove from the heat and set aside.

5   Place the pan with presoaked rice onto the stove top, adding a little extra water if necessary and bring it to the boil. Stir once, to separate the grains. Once boiling, continue to cook until the rice is 'al dente'. This process should take about 5–7 minutes, once the water has boiled. To test if the rice is ready for the next step, carefully remove a grain or two and bite through to the centre. The rice should be firm in the centre and soft on the outside. Strain the rice and rinse thoroughly under cool water.

6   Gently mix the parboiled rice together with the lamb and green bean mixture.

7   Return the empty pan to the stove top and add the canola oil. Once it is sizzling, add the turmeric and swirl gently to distribute and colour the oil. Spoon in the parboiled mixed rice. Form the rice into a mound and poke a few holes deep into the rice so the steam can circulate.

8   Mix the melted butter, liquid saffron and water together and pour some of it over the rice. Cover the pan with a clean tea towel and place the lid on the pan. Tie the ends of the tea towel together on top of the lid to prevent them from catching fire. After 30 seconds, turn the heat down to minimum and steam the rice for 45 minutes.

9   After 45 minutes, carefully remove the lid and check to see if the rice is fully cooked. If necessary, add a little more of the prepared saffron, butter and water mix. Place the lid back on and continue to cook for another 15 minutes.

10   To check if the tah dig is ready, wet your finger and quickly tap the side of the pan, approximately 3 cm from the base. If you see a sizzle and hear a small hiss, the tah dig is ready.

serving suggestion
Flip the rice onto a large flat tray Tip: Leaving the tah dig in the pan for a few minutes to cool slightly helps to release it from the pan. Serve with Greek-style, plain yoghurt and pickles.

serves 6   **prep** 30m   **soak** 1h   **cook** 2h 15m

rice
3 cups basmati rice
1 tbsp salt
pinch of turmeric

green bean mix
500 g fresh green beans
4 tbsp olive oil
1 large brown onion, finely chopped
1 tsp minced garlic
500 g lamb mince
1 tsp salt
½ tsp black pepper
½ tsp cinnamon
1 tbsp turmeric
1 tsp advieh polo*
4 dried limes
3 tbsp tomato purée
2 large tomatoes, diced
2 cups (500 ml) water

for cooking
¼ cup canola oil
¼ tsp turmeric
2 tbsp butter, melted
2 tsp liquid saffron*
¼ cup (60 ml) water

notes
*See page 20 for instructions on how to make advieh polo (spice blend for rice).
**See page 18 for instructions on how to make liquid saffron.

[pronounced / kal-aam pol-low]

kalam polo

RICE WITH MEATBALLS & CABBAGE

serves 6 **prep** 45m **soak** 1h **cook** 2h

rice
3 cups basmati rice
1 tbsp salt
½ tsp turmeric

meatballs
500 g beef mince
1 small brown onion, grated
1 tsp salt
½ tsp black pepper
½ tsp turmeric

sauce
4 tbsp olive oil
1 large brown onion, finely chopped
4 tbsp tomato purée
1 tsp salt
½ tsp black pepper
¼ tsp cinnamon
1 tbsp turmeric
2 cups (500 ml) water
1 small green cabbage
½ cup sultanas

tah dig (golden crust)
2 tbsp liquid saffron*
3 tbsp Greek-style, plain yoghurt

for cooking
¼ cup canola oil

note
*See page 18 for instructions
on how to make liquid saffron.

1   Rinse the rice thoroughly under running water, until the water runs clear. Transfer the rice into a large, heavy-based pan. Add the salt and enough water to cover the rice by about 10 cm. Soak for 1 hour. Note: Rinsing removes some of the starch from the rice, making it less susceptible to sticking together. The salt preserves the shape and adds flavour.

2   Combine the ingredients for the meatballs and form into small balls the size of hazelnuts. In a medium-sized, non-stick pan heat 2 tablespoons of the olive oil and fry the meatballs, in small batches until browned all over. Remove from the pan, drain on absorbent paper and set aside.

3   Reheat the pan, adding a little more oil if necessary and fry the onion over a medium heat until golden-brown. Add the tomato purée, salt, pepper, cinnamon, turmeric and water. Stir gently to combine. Return the meatballs to the pan, cover and simmer over a low heat, for 20 minutes.

4   Meanwhile, remove the core from the cabbage and cut into 2 cm pieces. Remove any hard, thick ribs and discard.

5   In a large, non-stick pan, heat the remaining olive oil and fry the cabbage over a medium heat for 10 minutes. Stir frequently, to prevent the cabbage from burning. Add the cabbage to the meatballs and stir through gently. Continue to cook for another 15 minutes, or until minimal liquid remains. Add the sultanas, stir through briefly, remove from the heat and set aside.

6   Place the pan with presoaked rice onto the stove top, adding a little extra water if necessary and bring it to the boil. Stir once, to separate the grains. Once boiling, continue to cook until the rice is 'al dente'. This process should take about 5—7 minutes, once the water has boiled. To test if the rice is ready for the next step, carefully remove a grain or two and bite through to the centre. The rice should be firm in the centre and soft on the outside. Strain the rice and rinse thoroughly under cool water.

7   In a small mixing bowl, mix 6 heaped tablespoons of the parboiled rice with the liquid saffron and yoghurt. This will create the tah dig.

8   Return the empty pan to the stove top and add the canola oil. Once it is sizzling, evenly spread the tah dig mixture over the bottom of the pan. Gently mix the remaining parboiled rice together with the cabbage and meatball mixture. Spoon the rice and cabbage mixture over the tah dig. Form the rice into a mound and poke a few holes deep into the rice so the steam can circulate.

9   Cover the pan with a clean tea towel and place the lid on the pan. Tie the ends of the tea towel together on top of the lid to prevent them from catching fire. After 30 seconds, turn the heat down to minimum and steam the rice for 1½ hours.

10   To check if the tah dig is ready, wet your finger and quickly tap the side of the pan, approximately 3 cm from the base. If you see a sizzle and hear a small hiss, the tah dig is ready.

serving suggestion
Spoon the rice onto a large flat tray and serve the tah dig on a separate plate. Sprinkle the rice with a little cinnamon and serve with Greek-style, plain yoghurt.

[pronounced / zer-esh-k po-low]

zereshk polo

BARBERRY RICE WITH SAFFRON CHICKEN

serves
6

prep
5m

soak
1h

cook
45m

3 cups basmati rice
1 tbsp salt

chicken sauce
4 tbsp olive oil
6 chicken pieces, with bone
2 large brown onions,
   finely chopped
1 cup (250 ml) water
2 tbsp lime juice
3 tbsp tomato purée
½ tsp salt
½ tsp black pepper
1 tbsp turmeric
2 tsp liquid saffron*

barberry sauce
2 tbsp olive oil
1 cup barberries*
1 tbsp sugar
2 tsp liquid saffron**
2 tbsp lime juice
2 tbsp water

for cooking
¼ cup canola oil
pinch of turmeric
1 tsp butter, melted

garnish
2 tbsp liquid saffron**
1 tbsp butter, melted

notes
*Barberries are a sour, dried fruit
available from Middle Eastern
specialty shops.
*See page 18 for instructions on how
to make liquid saffron.

1   Rinse the rice thoroughly under running water, until the water runs clear. Transfer the rice into a large, heavy-based pan. Add the salt and enough water to cover the rice by about 10 cm. Soak for 1 hour. Note: Rinsing removes some of the starch from the rice, making it less susceptible to sticking together. The salt preserves the shape and adds flavour.

2   In a large, non-stick pan, heat the olive oil and fry the chicken pieces over a medium heat until golden-brown. Remove the chicken from the pan and drain on absorbent paper.

3   Return the pan to the heat and fry the onion over a medium heat until golden-brown. Add the water, lime juice, tomato purée, salt, pepper, turmeric and liquid saffron. Return the chicken to the pan, cover and simmer over a low heat for 45 minutes.

4   Meanwhile in a small, non-stick pan, heat the olive oil and fry the barberries over a medium heat for 1 minute. Stir constantly as they burn easily. Add the sugar, liquid saffron, lime juice and water. Cook over a low heat for 2 minutes. Remove the pan from the heat and set aside.

5   Place the pan with presoaked rice onto the stove top, adding a little extra water if necessary and bring it to the boil. Stir once, to separate the grains. Once boiling, continue to cook until the rice is 'al dente'. This process should take about 5—7 minutes, once the water has boiled. To test if the rice is ready for the next step, carefully remove a grain or two and bite through to the centre. The rice should be firm in the centre and soft on the outside. Strain the rice and rinse thoroughly under cool water. This prevents the rice from cooking any further.

6   Return the empty pan to the stove top and add the canola oil. Once it is sizzling, add the turmeric and swirl gently to distribute and colour the oil. Mix three-quarters of the barberries through the parboiled rice before spooning into the pan. Form the rice into a mound and poke a few holes deep into the rice so the steam can circulate. Drizzle the melted butter over the rice and cover the pan with a clean tea towel. Place the lid on the pan and carefully tie the corners of the tea towel on top of the lid. After 30 seconds, turn the heat down to minimum and steam the rice for 1 hour.

7   To check if the tah dig is ready, wet your finger and quickly tap the side of the pan, approximately 3 cm from the base. If you see a sizzle and hear a small hiss, then the tah dig is ready.

serving suggestion
Spoon the rice onto a large flat tray, reserving 3—4 tablespoons of rice for the garnish. Mix the reserved rice together with the liquid saffron and melted butter and spoon over the top of the rice. Garnish with the remaining barberries. Serve the chicken and sauce separately.

tah chin esfanaj

LAMB, YOGHURT & SPINACH PILAF

1   In a large, non-stick pan, heat 2 tablespoons of the olive oil and fry the lamb in small batches, until browned all over. Add the water, salt, pepper, turmeric, cinnamon and paprika. Cover and simmer for 1½ hours. Note: At this stage the lamb should be almost cooked but not falling apart and minimal liquid should remain. With a slotted spoon, remove the meat from the pan. Transfer to a shallow dish and allow to cool. Save any remaining liquid for later.

2   Meanwhile, in a medium-sized, non-stick pan, heat the remaining olive oil and fry the onion over a medium heat until golden-brown. Add the garlic and spinach and continue to cook over a medium heat for 5 minutes, stirring occasionally. Remove from the heat and allow to cool slightly.

3   Mix the marinade ingredients together and pour over the lamb. Add the onions and spinach and mix well. Place in the refrigerator to marinate for 2 hours.

4   Meanwhile, inse the rice thoroughly under running water, until the water runs clear. Transfer the rice into a large, heavy-based pan. Add the salt, turmeric and enough water to cover the rice by about 10 cm. Soak for 1 hour. Note: Rinsing removes some of the starch from the rice, making it less susceptible to sticking together. The salt preserves the shape and adds flavour.

5   Place the pan with presoaked rice onto the stove top, adding a little extra water if necessary and bring it to the boil. Stir once, to separate the grains. Once boiling, continue to cook until the rice is 'al dente'. This process should take about 5—7 minutes, once the water has boiled. To test if the rice is ready for the next step, carefully remove a grain or two and bite through to the centre. The rice should be firm in the centre and soft on the outside. Strain the rice and rinse thoroughly under cool water. This prevents the rice from cooking any further, while you prepare the tah dig.

6   Squeeze any excess marinade from the lamb and spinach and reserve. Prepare the tah dig by mixing together 1 cup of the parboiled rice with the beaten egg, yoghurt, liquid saffron and excess marinade.

7   Return the empty pan to the stove top and add the canola oil. Once it is sizzling, line the bottom of the pan with the tah dig mixture. Spoon half of the parboiled rice over the tah dig, then add the lamb and spinach to create the middle layer. Finally spoon in the remaining rice. Use a wooden spoon to pack the rice down and pour the melted butter over the rice. Cover the pan with a clean tea towel and place the lid on the pan. Tie the ends of the tea towel together on top of the lid to prevent them from catching fire. After 30 seconds, turn the heat down to minimum and steam the rice for 1½ hours.

8   To check if the tah dig is ready, wet your finger and quickly tap the side of the pan, approximately 3 cm from the base. If you see a sizzle and hear a small hiss, then the tah dig is ready.

serving suggestion

To serve, remove the pan from the heat and allow to cool for 5 minutes, without removing the lid. After 5 minutes, carefully remove the lid and place a large, round tray over the pan. Hold firmly with both hands and flip the rice upside down onto the tray. Slice like a cake in to 6 evenly sized portions.

serves 6
prep 10m
soak 1h
cook 3h
+ 2h marinating

4 tbsp olive oil
2 kg stewing lamb, cut into
    2 cm cubes
6 cups (1½ litres) water
½ tsp salt
½ tsp black pepper
1 tsp turmeric
½ tsp cinnamon
½ tsp paprika
1 large brown onion, finely
    chopped
1 tsp minced garlic
2 cups spinach, finely chopped

marinade
1 cup Greek-style, plain yogurt
3 tbsp saffron liquid*
½ tsp salt
½ tsp black pepper
½ tsp cinnamon
½ tsp minced garlic

rice
3 cups basmati rice
1 tbsp salt
½ tsp turmeric

tah dig (golden crust)
1 egg, beaten
2 tbsp Greek-style, plain yoghurt
1 tsp liquid saffron

for cooking
¼ cup canola oil
2 tbsp butter, melted

note
*See page 18 for instructions on how to make liquid saffron.

tips
1 The rice should be approximately 3 cm high above and below the lamb and spinach centre.

2 It is important to use a large gas ring over the lowest heat setting. This ensures the heat is distributed evenly and does not burn the rice in one spot.

reshteh polo

RICE WITH NOODLES, SULTANAS & DATES

serves	prep	soak	cook
6	20m	1h	1h 20m

3 cups basmati rice
1 tbsp salt
pinch of turmeric
4 oranges
2 tbsp olive oil
2 onions, finely chopped
1 tbsp butter
½ cup sultanas
10 dried dates, roughly chopped
½ tsp salt
½ tsp black pepper
½ tsp turmeric
½ tsp cinnamon
1 tsp advieh polo*
500 g reshteh noodles**,
  broken into 3 cm lengths

tah dig (golden crust)
2 tbsp plain yoghurt
3 tsp liquid saffron***

for cooking
¼ cup canola oil

notes
*See page 20 for instructions on how to
make advieh polo (spice blend for rice).
**Reshteh are thin, round noodles
made from wheat. They are symbolic of
the unravelling of life's problems and
feature during Persian Noruz (New
Year) celebrations. Angel hair pasta,
capellini and linguini are all suitable
substitutes.
***See page 18 for instructions on how
to make liquid saffron.

1   Rinse the rice thoroughly under running water, until the water runs clear. Transfer the rice into a large, heavy-based pan. Add the salt, turmeric and enough water to cover the rice by about 10 cm. Soak for 1 hour. Note: Rinsing removes some of the starch from the rice, making it less susceptible to sticking together. The salt preserves the shape and adds flavour.

2   Remove the skin from the oranges using a vegetable peeler and cut into slivers the size of matchsticks. Try not to remove too much of the white, bitter pith. Place the orange slivers in a small pan of boiling water, simmer for 5 minutes before straining the water.

3   In a medium-sized, non-stick pan, heat the olive oil and fry the onion over a medium heat until golden-brown. Add the butter, sultanas, chopped dates and slivered orange peel. Continue to cook over a low heat for 2 minutes. Add the salt, pepper, turmeric, cinnamon and advieh polo. Stir through, remove from the heat and set aside.

4   Add the reshteh noodles to the pan with presoaked rice and place on the stove top. Add a little extra water if necessary and bring it to the boil. Stir once, to separate the grains. Once boiling, continue to cook until the rice is 'al dente'. This process should take about 5—7 minutes, once the water has boiled. To test if the rice is ready for the next step, carefully remove a grain or two and bite through to the centre. The rice should be firm in the centre and soft on the outside. Strain the rice and noodles and rinse thoroughly under cool water. This prevents the rice from cooking any further, while you prepare the tah dig.

5   Now prepare the tah dig. Take 6 heaped tablespoons of the parboiled rice and noodles and mix together with the yoghurt and liquid saffron.

6   Add the sultana and date mixture to the remaining parboiled rice and noodles, and gently mix.

7   Return the empty pan to the stove top and add the canola oil. Once it is sizzling, carefully spoon in the prepared tah dig mixture. Spoon the rice, noodle and sultana mixture over the tah dig and form into a mound. Poke a few holes deep into the rice so the steam can circulate. Cover the pan with a clean tea towel and place the lid on the pan. Tie the ends of the tea towel together on top of the lid to prevent them from catching fire. After 30 seconds, turn the heat down to minimum and steam the rice for 1½ hours.

8   To check if the tah dig is ready, wet your finger and quickly tap the side of the pan, approximately 3 cm from the base. If you see a sizzle and hear a small hiss, then the tah dig is ready.

serving suggestion
Spoon the rice onto a large, flat tray. Gently scrape the tah dig from the bottom of the pan and serve on a separate plate. Note: Leaving the tah dig in the pan for a few minutes to cool slightly helps release it from the pan. Serve with Greek-style, plain yoghurt, pickles and fresh herbs. See page 34 for information on suitable types of fresh herbs.

kebabs

The word 'kebab' literally means char-grilled or broiled meat, chicken or fish. In Iran, kebabs are commonly cooked over a hot charcoal barbecue.

They are mostly eaten in restaurants due to the technical skills needed in the preparation, as well as in the cooking. Marinades often contain minced onion, garlic, lime juice, saffron and occasionally yoghurt.

mostly kebabs

morgh-e shekam por

STUFFED ROAST CHICKEN

serves 6
prep 15m
soak 1h
cook 1h 45m

3 cups basmati rice
1 tbsp salt
1.5 kg fresh whole chicken

chicken stuffing
2 tbsp olive oil
1 large brown onion, finely chopped
1 tsp minced garlic
12 dried apricots, roughly chopped
6 pitted prunes, roughly chopped
¼ cup sultanas
1 large apple, peeled & diced
2 tbsp barberries*
1 tsp orange zest
¼ cup walnuts, roughly chopped
1 tbsp dried rose petals**
1 tsp salt
½ tsp black pepper
½ tsp cinnamon
½ tsp dried thyme
1 tsp advieh polo***
2 tsp liquid saffron****

basting sauce
1 tbsp melted butter
1 tbsp liquid saffron****
2 tbsp lime juice

tah dig (golden crust)
1 large pita bread

for cooking
¼ cup canola oil
¼ tsp turmeric
2 tbsp butter, melted
2 tsp liquid saffron****
¼ cup (60 ml) water

1   Rinse the rice thoroughly under running water, until the water runs clear. Transfer the rice into a large, heavy-based pan. Add the salt and enough water to cover the rice by about 10 cm. Soak for 1 hour. Note: Rinsing removes some of the starch from the rice, making it less susceptible to sticking together. The salt preserves the shape and adds flavour.

2   Preheat the oven to 190 ℃.

3   In a small, non-stick pan, heat the olive oil and fry the onion over a medium heat until golden-brown. Add the garlic, apricots, prunes, sultanas and apple. Fry for another minute. Remove the pan from the heat, add the remaining stuffing ingredients and mix well. Set aside to cool to room temperature.

4   Mix the basting sauce ingredients. Stuff the chicken with the dried fruit mixture. Place in an ovenproof dish and baste with the sauce. Loosely cover with aluminium foil and roast for 45 minutes.

5   Remove the chicken from the oven. Scoop out the stuffing and set aside. Return the chicken to the oven and roast, uncovered for another 35—45 minutes, occasionally basting with the pan juices. Once cooked, remove from the oven, cover with aluminium foil and allow to rest for 15 minutes. This allows the juices to settle, making the chicken easier to carve.

6   Meanwhile, place the pan with presoaked rice onto the stove top, adding a little extra water if necessary and bring it to the boil. Stir once, to separate the grains. Once boiling, continue to cook until the rice is 'al dente'. This process should take about 5—7 minutes, once the water has boiled. To test if the rice is ready for the next step, carefully remove a grain or two and bite through to the centre. The rice should be firm in the centre and soft on the outside. Strain the rice, rinse thoroughly under cool water and mix with the dried fruit stuffing.

7   Return the empty pan to the stove top and add the canola oil. Once it is sizzling, add the turmeric and swirl gently to distribute and colour the oil. Carefully place the bread on the bottom of the pan and spoon in the parboiled rice and dried fruit mixture. Form the rice into a mound and poke a few holes deep into the rice so the steam can circulate.

8   Mix the melted butter, liquid saffron and water together and pour some of it over the rice. Cover the pan with a clean tea towel and place the lid on the pan. Tie the ends of the tea towel together on top of the lid to prevent them from catching fire. After 30 seconds, turn the heat down to minimum and steam the rice for 45 minutes. After 45 minutes, carefully remove the lid, and check if the rice is fully cooked. If necessary, add a little more of the prepared saffron, butter and water mix. Place the lid back on and continue to cook for another 15 minutes.

9   To check if the tah dig is ready, wet your finger and quickly tap the side of the pan, approximately 3 cm from the base. If you see a sizzle and hear a small hiss, then the tah dig is ready.

serving suggestion
Spoon the rice onto a large, flat tray and garnish with the roast chicken. Gently scrape the tah dig from the bottom of the pan and serve on a separate plate. Tip: Leaving the tah dig in the pan for a few minutes to cool slightly helps to release it from the pan.

notes
*Barberries are dried, tart, sour berries that complement chicken dishes perfectly.
**Dried rose petals are optional but give a lovely, fragrant taste to the dish.
***See page 20 for instructions on how to make advieh polo (spice blend for rice).
****See page 18 for instructions on how to make liquid saffron.

tasty tip

For a juicier, more succulent chicken, remove it from the fridge 1 hour before cooking and allow it to reach room temperature.

tip

When wrapping the meat around the skewers, have a bowl of warm water handy to dip your hands in. This prevents the meat from sticking to your hands and assists in smoothing out the kebabs.

kebab koobideh

[pronounced / ke-bab koo-bee-deh]

LAMB MINCE SKEWERS

1   Prepare the charcoal barbecue. Place two firelighters onto the base of the barbecue. Stack charcoal briquettes in a pyramid shape over the firelighters. Light the firelighters and let the charcoal burn for about 30 minutes, or until glowing red hot. Use long-handled tongs to spread the charcoal evenly over the bottom of the barbecue and let the fire die down for a few minutes.

2   Meanwhile, squeeze any excess water from the grated onion. Combine the onion and lamb and beef mince together by hand until the mixture turns a pale colour and the fat is evenly distributed. Add the salt, pepper and turmeric and continue to mix, until all ingredients are thoroughly combined. Tip: You could also use a food processor in this step, but be sure to chill the bowl and blade first.

3   Wrap the meat mixture around the flat, 2 cm metal skewers (see tip on page 164). Start wrapping the mixture approximately 3 cm from the tip of the skewer, and shape it to the width of your barbecue. Squeeze the meat mixture firmly onto the skewers, making them as flat and uniform as possible. Mix together the basting sauce.

4   Thread the tomatoes onto the thin metal skewer, and place it over the hot coals. Cook until charred on the outside and heated through. Move to one side of the barbecue to keep warm while you cook the mince skewers.

5   Start by placing a few of the prepared kebab skewers over the hot coals. Turn the kebabs immediately and often to avoid the meat falling off the skewers. Note: It is important to have the coals hot enough, so the mince contracts and keeps the juice inside, but not too hot that they burn instantly. As you go, fan the flames from any dripping oil to prevent the outside from burning and baste with the sauce. Cook the skewers for a total of 3—4 minutes per side.

6   When the kebabs are ready, place a piece of kebab bread on a flat tray. Lay the kebab skewers on top of the bread, place a second piece of kebab bread over the skewers, firmly press down and pull the kebab from the skewers. Cover, with aluminium foil and continue cooking the remainder of the kebabs.

serving suggestion
Serve immediately with flatbread or steamed rice, char-grilled tomatoes and a sprinkling of sumac.

note
*Sumac is a coarse, sour spice that can be found in Middle Eastern specialty shops.

The photos to the right are of a famous kebab shop in Tajrish, which is located to the north of Tehran. The shop specialises in making the most delicious kebab koobideh.

They mince the meat and skewer the kebabs right in front of your eyes, so you know exactly what is going into your kebab.

You can see by the length of their barbecue how many kebabs they are capable of cooking during peak times. They also make delicious fresh kebab bread.

---

serves 4—6
prep 30m
cook 10m

1 large brown onion, grated
400 g fatty lamb mince
100 g fatty beef mince
1 tsp salt
½ tsp black pepper
pinch of turmeric

basting sauce
2 tbsp butter, melted
2 tbsp lime juice
1 tbsp tomato purée

to serve
4—6 Roma tomatoes
2 tbsp sumac*
fresh kebab bread

for cooking
8 x flat, 2 cm metal skewers
1 x thin, ½ cm metal skewer

[pronounced / sheesh-lik]

shishlik

MARINATED LAMB RIB CHOPS

serves	prep	marinate	cook
6	5m	12 - 24h	10m

12 lamb rib chops
4 Roma tomatoes

marinade
2 tsp liquid saffron*
2 tbsp Greek-style, plain yogurt
½ cup (125 ml) lime juice
1 tbsp lime zest
1 large brown onion, grated
½ tsp minced garlic
1 tsp salt
½ tsp black pepper

basting sauce
¼ cup butter
2 tsp liquid saffron*
2 tbsp lime juice
1 tsp salt
½ tsp black pepper

for cooking
2 x flat, 1 cm metal skewers
1 x thin, ½ cm metal skewer

1   Mix the marinade ingredients together. Place the lamb chops in a suitable container and pour the marinade over them. Using your hands, work the marinade into the chops. Cover the container and refrigerate overnight.

2   Prepare the charcoal barbecue. Place two firelighters onto the base of the barbecue. Stack charcoal briquettes in a pyramid shape over the firelighters. Light the firelighters and let the charcoal burn for about 30 minutes, or until glowing red hot. Use long-handled tongs to spread the charcoal evenly over the bottom of the barbecue and let the fire die down for a few minutes.

3   Meanwhile, prepare the basting sauce by melting the butter. Add the liquid saffron, lime juice, salt and pepper. Stir to mix, remove from the heat and set aside.

4   Thread the tomatoes onto the thin metal skewer. Place over the coals and cook until charred on the outside and heated through. Move to one side of the barbecue to keep warm while you cook the lamb skewers. Thread the lamb chops onto the flat, 1 cm skewers and place over the coals. As you go, fan the flames from any dripping oil to prevent the outside from burning. Cook the skewers for a total of 3—4 minutes per side. Turn the skewers and baste with the sauce regularly.

5   When the kebabs are ready, place a piece of kebab bread on a flat tray. Lay the skewers on top of the bread, place a second piece of kebab bread over the skewers, firmly press down and pull the meat from the skewers.

serving suggestion
Delicious served with steamed basmati rice and char-grilled tomatoes.

note
*See page 18 for instructions on how to make liquid saffron.

koofteh tabrizi

TABRIZ MEATBALLS

serves 4 | **prep** 20m | **cook** 2h 30m

meatballs

3 cups (750 ml) water
1 cup yellow split peas
½ cup basmati rice
500 g lamb mince
½ cup rice flour
2 eggs, lightly beaten
2 large brown onions, grated
1 cup fresh, flat-leaf parsley,
   finely chopped
1 leek, green-ends only, finely
   chopped
2 tbsp dried tarragon
1 tsp salt
½ tsp black pepper
½ tsp cinnamon
1 tsp turmeric

1   In a small saucepan, bring the water to the boil. Add the split peas and simmer for 15 minutes. Add the rice, bring the water back to the boil and simmer for a further 10 minutes. Strain and rinse under cool water.

2   In a large bowl, mix the lamb mince together with the rice flour, eggs and onion. Add the remaining meatball ingredients, along with the cooked split peas and rice. Mix well.

3   Divide the meat mixture into four equal-sized portions. Form into meatballs the size of oranges.

4   With your thumb, make a hole in the centre of each meatball. Place 2 prunes, 1 tsp of barberries, 1 walnut half, 1 dried apricot half and 1 tsp of fried onion into the holes. Close the opening and reshape the meatballs. Make sure the dried fruits and nuts end up in the centre of the meatballs.

continued on next page...

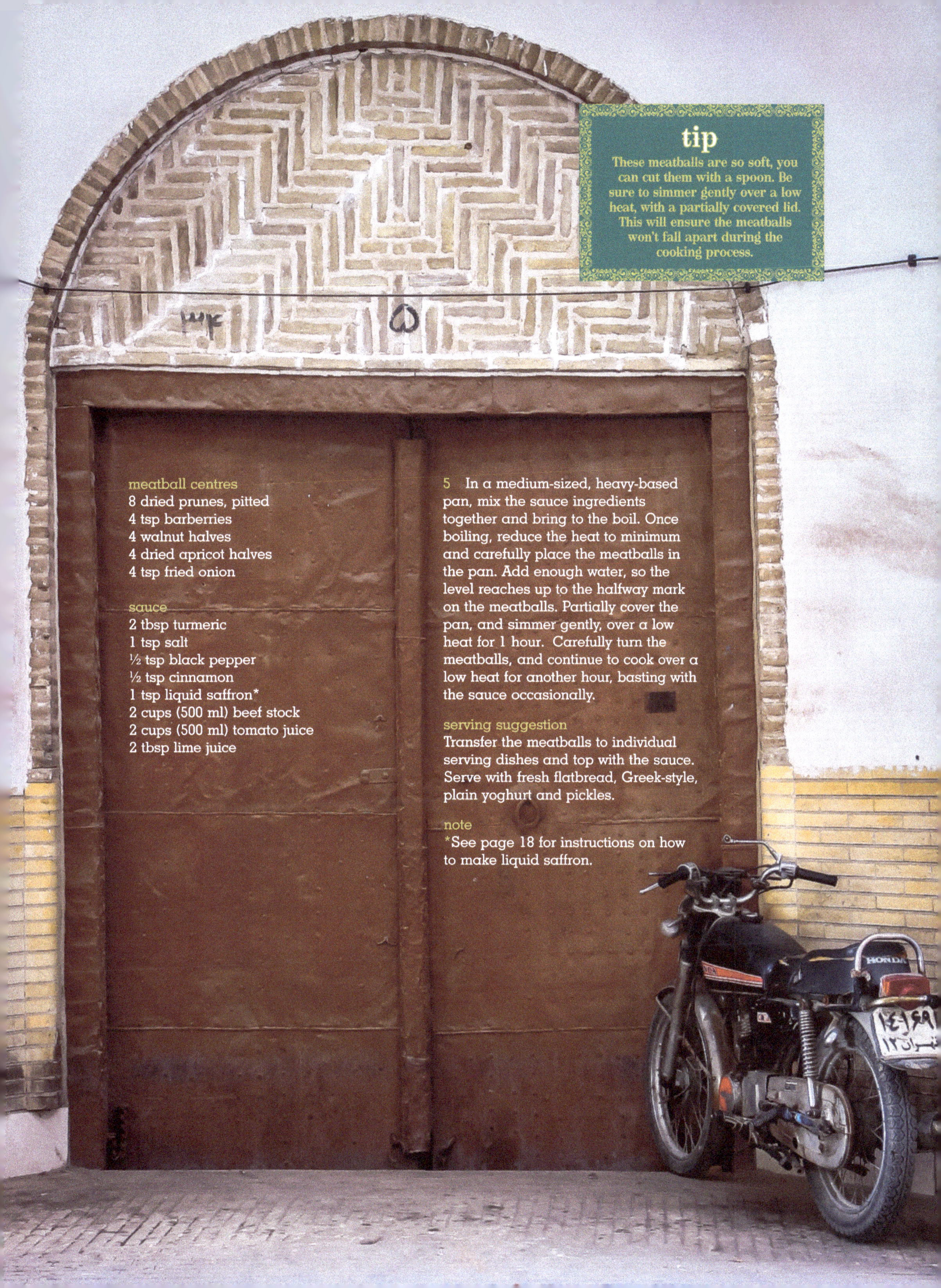

tip

These meatballs are so soft, you can cut them with a spoon. Be sure to simmer gently over a low heat, with a partially covered lid. This will ensure the meatballs won't fall apart during the cooking process.

meatball centres

8 dried prunes, pitted
4 tsp barberries
4 walnut halves
4 dried apricot halves
4 tsp fried onion

sauce

2 tbsp turmeric
1 tsp salt
½ tsp black pepper
½ tsp cinnamon
1 tsp liquid saffron*
2 cups (500 ml) beef stock
2 cups (500 ml) tomato juice
2 tbsp lime juice

5 In a medium-sized, heavy-based pan, mix the sauce ingredients together and bring to the boil. Once boiling, reduce the heat to minimum and carefully place the meatballs in the pan. Add enough water, so the level reaches up to the halfway mark on the meatballs. Partially cover the pan, and simmer gently, over a low heat for 1 hour. Carefully turn the meatballs, and continue to cook over a low heat for another hour, basting with the sauce occasionally.

serving suggestion

Transfer the meatballs to individual serving dishes and top with the sauce. Serve with fresh flatbread, Greek-style, plain yoghurt and pickles.

note

*See page 18 for instructions on how to make liquid saffron.

[pronounced / ke-bab oz-oon-br-oon]

kebab ozoonbroon

CHAR-GRILLED SALMON KEBABS

serves 4
prep 5m
marinate 30m
cook 10m

500 g salmon fillets, skin on,
  cut into 3 cm cubes
4 Roma tomatoes
1 small red capsicum, quartered

marinade
4 limes
2 tbsp olive oil
1 large brown onion, grated
1 tsp minced garlic
1 tsp salt
½ tsp black pepper

basting sauce
2 tbsp butter
½ cup lime juice
1 tsp tomato purée
½ tsp salt
½ tsp black pepper

for cooking
3 x flat, 1 cm metal skewers
2 x thin, ½ cm metal skewers

to serve
limes, halved
2 tbsp sumac*
lavash bread
baby spinach leaves

1   Remove the zest from the limes, cut in half and juice. Place the zest and juice in a mixing bowl, add the remaining marinade ingredients and mix well. Add the salmon cubes and marinate for 30 minutes.

2   Meanwhile, prepare the basting sauce. Melt the butter in a small saucepan. Add the lime juice, tomato purée, salt and pepper and bring to the boil. Remove from the heat and set aside.

3   Prepare the charcoal barbecue. Place two firelighters onto the base of the barbecue. Stack charcoal briquettes in a pyramid shape over the firelighters. Light the firelighters and let the charcoal burn for about 30 minutes, or until glowing red hot. Use long-handled tongs to spread the charcoal evenly over the bottom of the barbecue and let the fire die down for a few minutes.

4   Thread the tomatoes and capsicum onto the ½ cm metal skewers and place over the hot coals. Cook until charred on the outside and heated through. Move to one side of the barbecue to keep warm while you cook the salmon skewers.

5   Thread the salmon onto the 1 cm metal skewers and place over the hot coals. As you go, fan the flames from any dripping oil to prevent the outside from burning. Cook the skewers for a total of 3—4 minutes per side, turning frequently and basting as necessary.

6   When the kebabs are ready, place a piece of lavash bread on a flat tray. Lay the kebab skewers on top of the bread, place a second piece of lavash bread over the skewers. Firmly press down and pull the salmon from the skewers. Sprinkle with sumac and a squeeze of lime juice.

serving suggestion
Serve the salmon kebabs with the char-grilled tomatoes and capsicum, fresh baby spinach leaves, flatbread, lime juice and a sprinkling of sumac.

note
*Sumac is a coarse, sour spice that can be found in Middle Eastern specialty shops.

tasty tip

If available, buy salmon with the skin on. It holds better on the skewers and becomes beautifully crisp when cooked over hot coals.

tip

Be sure to marinate for at least 12 hours; the longer, the better. Also, let the meat rest for 5 minutes before serving. This allows the juices to settle and results in softer meat. Finally, do not overcook.

chenjeh kebab

MARINATED LAMB KEBABS

1   Make small incisions on both sides of the lamb with a sharp knife. Transfer to an airtight container with a lid. Note: Making small incisions helps the marinade penetrate into the meat.

2   Mix the marinade ingredients together and pour over the lamb. With your fingers, thoroughly work the marinade into the meat. Allow to marinate for at least 12 hours, turning once or twice to ensure even marination.

3   Prepare the charcoal barbecue. Place two firelighters onto the base of the barbecue. Stack charcoal briquettes in a pyramid shape over the firelighters. Light the firelighters and let the charcoal burn for about 30 minutes, or until glowing red hot. Use long-handled tongs to spread the charcoal evenly over the bottom of the barbecue and let the fire die down for a few minutes.

4   Meanwhile, prepare the basting sauce. Melt the butter in a small saucepan. Add the lime juice, liquid saffron and pepper and bring to the boil. Remove from the heat and set aside.

5   Thread the lamb onto the flat, 1 cm metal skewers. Make the length of your kebabs fit with the width of your barbecue.

6   Thread the tomatoes onto the thin, ½ cm metal skewer and place it over the hot coals. Cook until charred on the outside and heated through. Move to one side of the barbecue to keep warm while you cook the kebab skewers.

7   Place a few of the prepared kebab skewers over the hot coals. Note: It is important to have the coals hot enough, so the meat contracts and keeps the juice inside, but not too hot that they burn instantly. As you go, fan the flames from any dripping oil to prevent the outside from burning. Cook the skewers for a total of 3—4 minutes per side. Turn occasionally and baste with the sauce as necessary.

8   When the kebabs are ready, place a piece of kebab bread on a flat tray. Lay the kebab skewers on top of the bread, place a second piece of kebab bread over the skewers, firmly press down and pull the lamb from the skewers. Cover with aluminium foil and continue cooking the remainder of the kebabs.

serving suggestion
Serve with flatbread, char-grilled tomatoes, lime juice and a sprinkling of sumac.

notes
*See page 18 for instructions on how to make liquid saffron.
**Sumac is a coarse, sour spice that can be found in Middle Eastern specialty shops.

serves 4 **prep** 5m **marinate** 12–48h **cook** 10m

500 g cubed lamb
4 Roma tomatoes

marinade
2 tbsp olive oil
1 large brown onion, minced
1 tsp minced garlic
½ cup (125 ml) lime juice
1 tsp salt
½ tsp black pepper
1 tbsp Greek-style, plain yoghurt
2 tsp liquid saffron*

basting sauce
2 tbsp butter
2 tbsp lime juice
1 tbsp liquid saffron*
½ tsp black pepper

for cooking
4 x flat, 1 cm metal skewers
1 x thin, ½ cm metal skewer

to serve
limes, halved
1 tbsp sumac**
flatbread

[pronounced / kot-let-eh]

kotleteh

LAMB PATTIES

500 g lamb mince
1 small brown onion, grated
2 eggs
1 small potato, grated
1 tsp lime zest
1 tsp salt
½ tsp black pepper
¼ tsp cinnamon
½ tsp turmeric
1 tsp minced garlic

for cooking
¼ cup canola oil

1   Combine all the
ingredients thoroughly, and
shape into round or oval
patties about 5 cm in
diameter, by 1 cm thick.

2   Heat the oil in a large,
non-stick pan and fry the
patties over a low to medium
heat for 4—5 minutes per
side, or until cooked through.
Alternatively, they can be
cooked on a preheated
barbecue plate.

serving suggestion
Serve with finely sliced
gherkin, onion, lettuce and
tomato.

tip

If quinces are unavailable, you can substitute them with green cooking apples. If using apples, add them in the final hour of cooking along with the potatoes and carrots.

tas kebab

AUTUMN POT ROAST

1 Pierce the lamb with a sharp knife several times, and insert the sliced garlic into the slits. Mix the lamb dusting ingredients together, and rub over the entire leg.

2 Heat the olive oil in a large, heavy-based pan and fry the lamb over a medium heat until browned all over. Briefly, remove the lamb from the pan and set aside.

3 Line the bottom of the same pan with the sliced onion.

4 Wash and core the quince but do not peel. It is very important to remove the core as it is too hard to eat, even after cooking. Cut the quince into quarters. Arrange the quinces, eggplants and dried apricots over the onions. Place the lamb leg on top.

5 Mix the sauce ingredients together and pour over the lamb. Cover, and simmer over a low heat for 3 hours, basting the lamb with the sauce occasionally.

6 Add the potatoes and carrots, and continue to cook for another 45 minutes. Finally, add the tomatoes and cook for another 15 minutes.

serving suggestion
Serve with steamed green vegetables.

notes
*See page 20 for instructions on how to make advieh khorosht (spice blend for stews).
**Verjuice is the unfermented juice from unripened grapes. It is available from Middle Eastern speciality shops.
***See page 18 for instructions on how to make liquid saffron.

serves 6 | **prep** 10m | **cook** 4h

2 kg leg of lamb
3 cloves garlic, thinly sliced
2 tbsp olive oil

lamb dusting
4 tbsp flour
1 tsp salt
½ tsp black pepper
½ tsp turmeric
¼ tsp cinnamon

autumn produce
3 large brown onions, thinly sliced
2 quinces
4 thin eggplants, peeled
6 dried apricots
4 small potatoes, halved
4 small carrots, peeled and halved
2 Roma tomatoes, halved

sauce
¼ cup (60 ml) water
1 tsp advieh khorosht*
2 tbsp verjuice**
3 tbsp tomato purée
2 tbsp liquid saffron***

Quince are an ancient, autumn fruit which grow on small trees, quite similar to apples. They are not at all well known and are usually quite hard to find.

The fruit, irregular in shape, has a yellow, fuzzy skin with whitish inner flesh. It is astringent, hard and almost inedible when raw, but once cooked is a totally different story.

Once cooked, the hard, inedible flesh becomes soft and changes into a beautiful, reddish-pink colour with an amazing perfume.

These meatballs are so soft, you can cut them with a spoon. Be sure to simmer gently over a low heat, with a partially covered lid. This will ensure the meatballs won't fall apart during the cooking process.

[pronounced / koof-teh ber-enj]

koofteh berenj

RICE MEATBALLS

serves
6

prep
30m

cook
2h

meatballs
3 cups (750 ml) water
½ cup yellow split peas
¾ cup basmati rice
500 g lamb mince
1 large brown onion, grated
1 tbsp minced garlic
3 eggs, beaten
½ cup fresh, flat-leaf parsley, finely chopped
¼ cup dried dill
1 tbsp dried tarragon
1 tsp salt
½ tsp black pepper
½ tsp turmeric
1 tsp advieh khorosht*

sauce
4 cups (1 litre) water
2 tsp liquid saffron**
2 tbsp lemon juice
1 tbsp turmeric
1 tbsp tomato purée
1 tsp salt
½ tsp black pepper

1   In a small saucepan, bring the water to the boil. Add the split peas and simmer for 15 minutes. Add the rice, bring the water back to the boil and simmer for another 15 minutes. Strain and rinse under cool water.

2   Mix the lamb mince together with the onion, garlic and beaten eggs. Add the cooked split peas and rice, along with the remaining meatball ingredients. Knead for a few minutes to ensure all ingredients are thoroughly combined. Form into meatballs the size of oranges.

3   In a large, heavy-based pan, mix the sauce ingredients together and bring to the boil. Once boiling, lower the heat to minimum and carefully place in the meatballs. Partially cover the pan with a lid and simmer gently over a low heat, for 1 hour. Carefully turn the meatballs and continue to cook over a low heat for another 30 minutes, basting with the sauce occasionally.

serving suggestion
Transfer the meatballs to individual serving dishes and spoon over the sauce. Serve with fresh flatbread, Greek-style, plain yoghurt and pickles.

notes
*See page 20 for instructions on how to make advieh khorosht (spice blend for stews).
**See page 18 for instructions on how to make liquid saffron.

[pronounced / taa-beh keb-ab]

tabeh kebab

PAN-FRIED KEBAB

1   In a large, non-stick pan, mix the onion together with the lamb mince, salt, pepper, garlic and turmeric until well combined.

2   Flatten the mixture with your hands and use a spatula to make deep lines, across the width of the pan. The lines should be approximately
3 cm wide and similar to the width of a kebab. Drizzle with 1 tablespoon of the olive oil, place the pan on the stove top, cover and cook over a medium heat for 10 minutes.

3   Spread half of the tomato purée on top of the kebab and add the water to the pan. Cover and cook for another 10 minutes.

4   With tongs and a spatula, carefully turn the kebabs over, one at a time. Spread the remaining tomato purée on top of the kebabs and place the tomato slices on top. Drizzle with the remaining olive oil, cover and continue to cook for another 10 minutes.

serving suggestion
Serve hot with flatbread, Greek-style, plain yoghurt and fresh herbs.
(See page 34, for information on suitable types of fresh herbs.)

serves 4 | prep 10m | cook 30m

1 large brown onion, grated
500 g lamb mince
1 tsp salt
½ tsp black pepper
½ tsp minced garlic
½ tsp turmeric
2 tbsp olive oil
3 tbsp tomato purée
1 cup (250 ml) water
2 tomatoes, sliced thickly

quick tip

As a great time-saving tip these patties can be made days ahead of time. Simply follow the recipe up to step 4 and freeze. Then thaw and cook as required.

[pronounced / shaa-mee]

shami

SPLIT PEA PATTIES

1   In a small saucepan, bring the water and salt to the boil. Add the split peas and simmer over a low heat for 30 minutes. Strain, rinse under cool water and mash.

2   Meanwhile, make the garlic-yoghurt sauce. Mix the ingredients together and refrigerate until needed.

3   In a large bowl, thoroughly combine the beef and lamb minces with the grated onion and garlic. Add the spices, eggs, cooked split peas and liquid saffron. Mix thoroughly, cover with cling wrap and refrigerate for 30 minutes.

4   Shape the mixture into oval or round patties about 5 cm in diameter by 1 cm thick. If the mixture gets too sticky, have a bowl of warm water to occasionally dip your hands in.

5   Heat the canola oil in a large, non-stick pan and fry the patties over a low to medium heat, for 4–5 minutes per side. The mixture is quite soft, so try to turn the patties only once, to avoid breaking.

serving suggestion
Serve with fresh flatbread, sliced gherkins, tomato, and the garlic-yoghurt sauce.

note
*See page 18 for instructions on how to make liquid saffron.

serves	prep	chill	cook
6	5m	30m	40m

2 cups (500 ml) water
½ tsp salt
½ cups yellow split peas
250 g beef mince
500 g lamb mince
1 large brown onion, grated
1 tsp minced garlic
1 tsp salt
½ tsp black pepper
½ tsp cinnamon
½ tsp paprika
1 tsp turmeric
1 tsp cumin
2 eggs, beaten
2 tsp liquid saffron*

garlic-yoghurt sauce
½ cup Greek-style, plain yoghurt
1 tbsp minced garlic
2 tbsp lime juice
1 tsp salt
½ tsp black pepper

for cooking
½ cup canola oil

[pronounced / toarsh shaa-mee]

torsh shami

TANGY LAMB & TOMATO MEATBALLS

serves 6

prep 15m

cook 1h

meatballs
2 eggs, beaten
¼ cup breadcrumbs
1 tsp baking powder
¼ cup (60 ml) milk
1 tsp salt
½ tsp black pepper
½ tsp minced garlic
1 large brown onions, grated
500 g lamb mince

sauce
3 tbsp tomato purée
4 tbsp lemon juice
1 tsp salt
½ tsp black pepper
½ tsp cinnamon
1 cup (250 ml) water

for cooking
¼ cup canola oil

1   In a large bowl, mix the eggs together with the breadcrumbs, baking powder, milk, salt, pepper and garlic. Add the onions and lamb mince and knead until all ingredients are thoroughly combined. Form the mixture into meatballs the size of small mandarins. Flatten each meatball slightly and poke a hole into the centre of both sides. Note: The holes ensure the meatballs cook evenly.

2   Heat the oil in a frying pan and fry the meatballs over a medium heat, until lightly browned on both sides. Remove from the pan and drain on absorbent paper.

3   Wipe any excess oil from the pan, add the sauce ingredients, mix together and bring to the boil.

4   Once boiling, lower the heat to minimum and carefully place the meatballs in the pan. Cover and simmer over a low heat, for 45 minutes, turning the meatballs occasionally.

serving suggestion
Serve with creamy, mashed potato and a fresh garden salad or flatbread and Greek-style, plain yoghurt.

mahi sefid

STUFFED WHOLE FISH

1 Preheat the oven to 200 °C.

2 Have your fishmonger gut and descale the fish. Rinse under cold water and pat dry with paper towel. Sprinkle the inside cavity with the salt.

3 Place the fish on a baking tray covered with aluminium foil. Make deep, diagonal cuts across the width of the fish. Do this on both sides, approximately 4 cm apart. Push a little of the sliced garlic and butter into the cuts and set aside.

4 In a medium-sized, non-stick pan, heat the olive oil and fry the onion over a medium heat until golden-brown. Add the garlic and cook for another minute. Add the remaining stuffing ingredients and continue to cook for 2 minutes. Remove from the heat and allow to cool to room temperature.

5 Stuff the fish with the mixture and pin the cavity shut with toothpicks. Dot the fish with a little extra liquid saffron and butter and wrap the fish tightly in aluminium foil. Place the fish in the oven and bake for 30—35 minutes. The fish should flake easily with a fork when cooked.

6 Meanwhile, prepare the barberry garnish. Heat the oil in a small frying pan and add the barberries, lime juice and liquid saffron. Cook over a low heat for 1 minute. Remove from the heat and set aside.

serving suggestion

Delicious served with baked paprikas, lime wedges, Greek-style, plain yoghurt and plenty of fresh flatbread.

notes

*Barberries are tart, dried berries that are available from Middle Eastern specialty shops.
**See page 18 for instructions on how to make liquid saffron.

---

serves 6 | **prep** 15m | **cook** 45m

1.5 kg whole barramundi, or any similar white fish
1 tsp salt
2 cloves garlic, sliced
80 g butter, roughly chopped

fish stuffing

2 tbsp olive oil
1 large brown onion, finely chopped
1 tsp minced garlic
¼ cup fresh mint, finely chopped
½ cup fresh, flat-leaf parsley, finely chopped
1 tbsp dried tarragon
¼ cup fresh coriander, finely chopped
1 cup walnuts, lightly toasted and finely chopped
½ cup barberries*
¼ cup (60 ml) lime juice
1 tsp salt
½ tsp black pepper
2 tbsp liquid saffron**

garnish

1 tsp olive oil
3 tbsp barberries*
1 tbsp lime juice
1 tbsp liquid saffron**

joojeh kebab

SAFFRON & LIME CHICKEN WINGS

serves 6 · **prep** 5m · **marinate** 12h · **cook** 10m

1 cup (250 ml) water
½ tsp turmeric
1 kg chicken wings
4 Roma tomatoes

marinade
2 tbsp olive oil
2 tbsp lime zest
½ cup (125 ml) lime juice
1 large brown onion, grated
1 tsp minced garlic
2 tbsp Greek-style, plain yoghurt
2 tsp liquid saffron*
1 tsp salt
½ tsp black pepper

basting sauce
2 tbsp butter, melted
2 tbsp lime juice
1 tsp liquid saffron*
½ tsp black pepper
½ tsp paprika
1 tsp chicken seasoning

for cooking
6 x flat, 1 cm metal skewers
1 x thin, ½ cm metal skewer

to serve
flatbread
lime wedges

note
*See page 18 for instructions on how to make liquid saffron.

1   Cut the chicken wings into three sections: wingettes, drumettes and wing-tips. Do this by using the heel of your knife, to cut through the cartilage, between the bones of the joints. For joojeh kebab, we are only interested in the wingettes and drumettes. Save and freeze the wing-tips for the next time you make chicken stock.

2   In a large frying pan, bring the water to the boil. Add the turmeric and chicken wingettes and drumettes. Cook over a medium heat for 5 minutes or until almost no water remains. Remove from the heat and allow to cool before transferring to an airtight container with a lid.

3   Mix the marinade ingredients together and pour over the chicken. With your fingers, thoroughly work the marinade into the meat. Allow it to marinate for at least 12 hours, turning once or twice to ensure even marination.

3   Prepare the charcoal barbecue. Place two firelighters onto the base of the barbecue. Stack charcoal briquettes in a pyramid shape over the firelighters. Light the firelighters and let the charcoal burn for about 30 minutes, or until glowing red hot. Use long-handled tongs to spread the charcoal evenly over the bottom of the barbecue and let the fire die down for a few minutes.

4   Meanwhile, combine the ingredients for the basting sauce.

5   Thread the tomatoes onto the ½ cm metal skewer, and place it over the hot coals. Cook until charred on the outside and heated through. Move to one side of the barbecue to keep warm while you cook the chicken skewers.

6   Thread the chicken onto the 1 cm skewers. Make the length of your kebabs fit the width of your barbecue. Start by placing a few of the prepared chicken skewers over the hot coals. Note: It is important to have the coals hot enough, so the chicken contracts and keeps the juice inside, but not too hot that it burns instantly. As you go, fan the flames from any dripping oil to prevent the outside from burning. Cook the skewers for a total of 3—4 minutes per side. Turn occasionally and baste with the sauce as necessary. The chicken juices will run clear when fully cooked.

7   When the kebabs are ready, place a piece of kebab bread on a flat tray. Lay the kebab skewers on top of the bread, place a second piece of kebab bread over the skewers, firmly press down and pull the chicken from the skewers. Cover with aluminium foil and continue cooking the remainder of the kebabs.

serving suggestion
Serve with warmed flatbread, char-grilled tomatoes and lime wedges.

variation

Boneless chicken thighs can also be used. Flatten the thighs a little with a mallet and then cut into 2 cm x 4 cm chunks. If using boneless thighs, there is no need to precook in water first.

tip

Whole, shelled almonds can be easily ground in a food processor. Pulse on and off a few times to ensure you end up with evenly chopped almonds. Try not to use blanched almonds because the skin of nuts is rich in antioxidants.

kotleteh morgh

CHICKEN & ALMOND PATTIES

1   Combine the ingredients for the patties together until the mixture is evenly mixed. Shape into round or oval patties, approximately 5 cm in diameter by1 cm thick.

2   In a small bowl, prepare the egg wash by lightly beating the eggs together with the liquid saffron, garlic, salt and pepper.

3   In a separate bowl mix the flour together with the turmeric and chicken salt. Dip the patties into the flour mix, and lightly coat both sides.

4   Meanwhile, mix the sauce ingredients together and refrigerate until needed.

5   Heat the canola oil in a large, non-stick pan. Dip each floured patty into the beaten egg mixture, and then carefully place in the oil. Fry the patties over a medium heat, for 4—5 minutes per side, or until cooked through.

serving suggestion
Serve with the coriander sauce, finely sliced gherkins, onion, tomato and fresh flatbread.

note
*See page 18 for instructions on how to make liquid saffron.

serves 6 | **prep** 15m | **cook** 10m

patties
½ cup ground almonds
500 g chicken mince
1 large brown onion, grated
1 tsp salt
½ tsp black pepper
1 tsp minced garlic
4 tbsp fresh flat-leaf parsley, finely chopped
1 egg

egg wash
3 eggs
1 tsp liquid saffron*
½ tsp minced garlic
½ tsp salt
½ tsp black pepper

flour coating
½ cup flour
pinch of turmeric
1 tsp chicken salt

coriander sauce
1 bunch fresh coriander, finely chopped
juice and zest of 1 lime
½ tsp minced garlic
2 tbsp Greek-style, plain yoghurt
1 tsp salt
½ tsp black pepper

for cooking
½ cup canola oil

torshi

Torsh is the Persian word for 'sour' and Torshi means pickled. Persians are extremely fond of their pickles and serve them alongside most main meals.

Traditionally the idea of pickling came about as a way of preserving fruits and vegetables when they were in season and abundant.

pickles & relishes

torshi makhloot

MIXED VEGETABLE PICKLE

makes 3 litres **prep** 2h 30m **cook** 10m

1 small cauliflower
250 g green beans
3 Lebanese cucumbers
3 green capsicums, deseeded
½ small celery
6 large carrots, peeled
250 g pickling onions
½ cup fresh mint leaves
½ cup fresh coriander
½ cup fresh, flat-leaf parsley
½ cup fresh chives
1 kg thin eggplants
2 litres wine vinegar
20 cloves garlic
1 tbsp turmeric
2 tbsp salt
1 tsp peppercorns
2 tsp advieh torshi*
1 tbsp dried tarragon
6 red chillies

1   Wash the cauliflower and break into individual florets. Cut the tips and tails from the green beans and chop into 2 cm lengths. Wash the cucumbers and capsicums and chop into 2 cm, bite-sized pieces. Wash the celery and chop into 2 cm lengths. Chop the carrots and onions into 2 cm, bite-sized pieces.

2   Wash and finely chop the mint, coriander, parsley and chives. Spread the chopped herbs over a tray and sprinkle with 1 tsp of salt. Cover with a clean tea towel and leave to air dry for 2 hours.

3   Meanwhile, chop the eggplants into 2 cm, bite-sized pieces. Heat the vinegar in a large soup pan. Add the eggplant and garlic and bring to the boil. Once boiling, reduce the heat and simmer for 10 minutes. Add the turmeric, salt, peppercorns, advieh torshi, tarragon and chillies. Remove from the heat and allow to cool.

4   Sterilise the jars by washing them thoroughly with soapy water, drying, then placing in a hot oven for 10 minutes.

5   In a large mixing bowl, combine all ingredients and mix thoroughly. Pack the pickles into the clean glass jars right to the brim. Seal and store in a cool, dry place for at least 2 months before using. Refrigerate after opening.

note
*See instructions on how to make advieh torshi (spice blend for pickles) on page 20.

mixed vegetable pickle

liteh

MIXED VEGETABLE RELISH

makes 2 litres | **prep** 2h 30m | **cook** 1h

½ cup fresh mint leaves
½ cup fresh coriander
½ cup fresh, flat-leaf parsley
1 large eggplant
6 large carrots, peel & grated
½ cauliflower
½ green cabbage
½ small celery
2 green capsicums, deseeded
1 tsp dried dill
2 tbsp minced garlic
1.5 litres wine vinegar
1 tbsp turmeric
½ tsp chilli flakes
1 tsp advieh torshi*
1 tbsp salt
½ tsp black pepper

1   Wash and finely chop the mint, coriander and parsley. Spread the chopped herbs over a tray and sprinkle with 1 teaspoon of salt. Cover with a clean tea towel and leave to air dry for 2 hours.

2   Preheat the oven to 180 ℃.

3   Place the eggplant on a gas burner over high heat, occasionally turning, until the skin is blackened and charred. This step is optional but imparts a beautiful, smoky flavour to the eggplant. If omitting this step prick, the eggplant several times with a fork to prevent it bursting in the oven.

4   Wrap the eggplant in aluminium foil, place in an ovenproof dish and bake for 1 hour. Remove from the oven and allow to cool, before removing and discarding the blackened skin and mashing the flesh.

5   Sterilise the jars by washing them thoroughly with soapy water, drying then placing them in a hot oven for 10 minutes.

6   Use a food processor to finely chop the cauliflower, cabbage, celery and capsicums.

7   Place the eggplant, carrot and finely chopped ingredients into a large bowl. Add the dill, garlic and spices and mix thoroughly.

8   Transfer the mixture to the clean glass jars and fill to the brim with vinegar. Stir the contents of the jar to ensure the vinegar is distributed evenly. Seal and store in a cool, dry place for at least 2 weeks before using. Refrigerate after opening.

note
*See instructions on how to make advieh torshi (spice blend for pickles) on page 20.

Torshi bademjoon is a delicious, easy-to-make pickle.

As with all pickles, buy eggplants when they are in season, cheap and abundant. Don't worry if the eggplants have a few blemishes; you won't see them in the finished product.

Always use the long, thin eggplant variety for this recipe if you can source them.

[pronounced / toar-shee bod-em-joon]

torshi bademjoon

EGGPLANT PICKLE

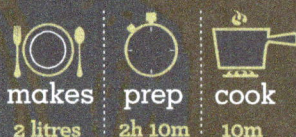

makes 2 litres **prep** 2h 10m **cook** 10m

15 long, thin eggplants
2 tbsp salt
1 litre vinegar
2 cups fresh mint leaves
1 cup fresh coriander
1 cup fresh, flat leaf parsley
½ cup fresh chives
20 garlic cloves, finely chopped
1 tbsp dried tarragon
1 tbsp turmeric
1 tbsp advieh torshi*
1 tbsp black mustard seeds
½ tsp black pepper
1 tbsp chilli flakes

1   Sterilise the jars by washing them thoroughly with soapy water, drying then placing them in a hot oven for 10 minutes.

2   Cut a lengthwise slit, on one side of each eggplant. Place the eggplants in a large pan with 1 tablespoon of salt and the vinegar. Bring to the boil and simmer gently for 10 minutes. Remove the eggplants from the pan, save the vinegar and set aside to cool and dry.

3   Meanwhile, wash and finely chop the mint, coriander, parsley and chives. Spread the chopped herbs on a tray and sprinkle with the remaining 1 tablespoon of salt. Cover with a clean tea towel and leave to air-dry for 2 hours.

4   Mix together the finely chopped garlic with the air-dried herbs. Add the dried tarragon, turmeric, advieh torshi, black mustard seeds, pepper and chilli flakes and mix thoroughly.

5   Stuff the cooled eggplants with the herb mixture and press to close. Place into the sterilised jars and fill to the brim with the saved vinegar. Store in a cool, dry place for at least 3 months before using. Refrigerate after opening.

serving suggestion
Cut into 2 cm rounds and present in a small dish.

note
*See instructions on how to make advieh torshi (spice blend for pickles) on page 20.

seer torshi

[pronounced / seer tor-sh-ee]

GARLIC PICKLE

1 Sterilise the jars by washing them thoroughly with soapy water, drying then placing in a hot oven for 10 minutes.

2 Meanwhile, remove the first, dry, outer layer of skin from each garlic bulb. Leave them whole and do not break into cloves. Place the bulbs into the sterilised jar.

3 Bring the vinegar and salt to the boil. Once boiling, remove from the heat. Set aside and allow to cool to room temperature before pouring over the garlic cloves.

4 Cover the lid with cling film and seal tightly. Write the date on the lid and place the jar in a cool, dark place.

5 After 3 months, check to see if you need to add any extra vinegar as the garlic will absorb some of the vinegar. They will be ready to serve after 12 months.

serving suggestion
Serve alongside your favourite Persian dish. Pickled garlic often accompanies dishes containing fish, eggplant and dill.

makes	prep	cook
1 litre	15m	5m

10 garlic bulbs
2½ cups (625 ml) malt vinegar
2 tbsp salt

In Iran, seer torshi is always eaten with fish as the taste of the mellow garlic perfectly complements the oiliness of the fish.

It is necessary to peel the garlic before eating, but the skin becomes very soft, making it easy to do so.

Due to the lengthy period of pickling the garlic has very little smell, making it quite easy to consume at least six cloves without worrying about garlic breath.

The photo to the right is a shop display of beautiful, crispy, golden smoked fish.

shirini

'Shirini' is the Persian word for all things sweet. Unlike the European custom, Persians are not great believers in having desserts like puddings or cakes after a meal.

The following recipes are a small collection of some of the more famous Persian sweets and are well worth trying.

sweet endings

[pronounced / show-leh zaar-d]

sholeh zard

SWEET SAFFRON PUDDING

1   Rinse the rice thoroughly under running water until the water runs clear. Pour the rice into a large, heavy-based pan. Place the pan on the stove top, add the water and sugar and bring to the boil.

2   Add the canola oil, liquid saffron, rosewater, cardamom and almonds. Stir through the rice. Cover and simmer over a low heat for 2 hours, stirring occasionally.

3   Transfer the cooked rice mixture to a serving dish of your choice and allow to cool to room temperature. Once cool, place in the refrigerator for 2 hours to chill. Just before serving, decorate with the cinnamon, almond and pistachio slivers.

serving suggestion
Serve chilled.

note
*See page 18 for instructions on how to make liquid saffron.

serves 6 | prep 10m | cook 2h | chill 2h

1 cup basmati rice
10 cups (2.5 litres) water
1 cup sugar
2 tbsp canola oil
3 tbsp liquid saffron*
½ cup (125 ml) rosewater
1 tsp ground cardamom
2 tbsp slivered almonds

garnish
1 tsp cinnamon
2 tsp almond slivers
2 tsp pistachio slivers

Photos to the right are of the huge copper vats used to distil rosewater and the famous Gol Mohammadi rose which is native to Iran.

The best rosewater in Iran is made in Kashan.

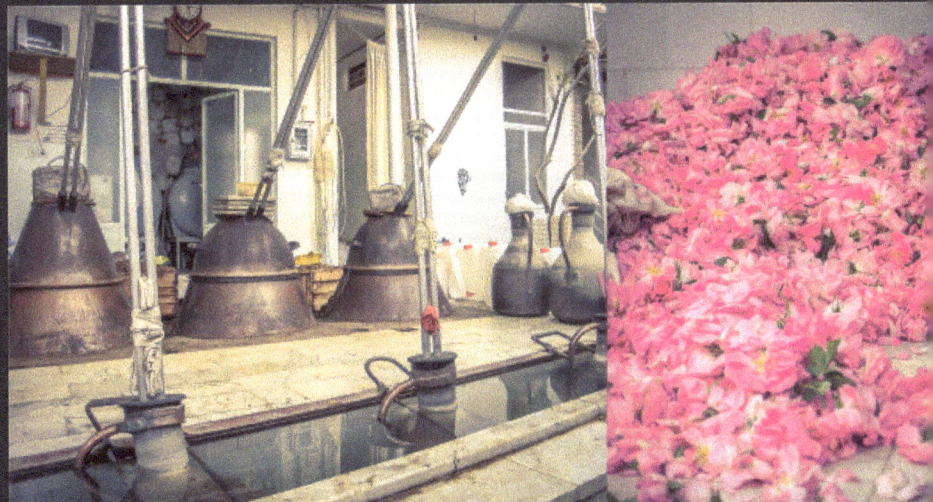

zoolbia

SPIRALS IN ROSEWATER SYRUP

serves | prep | cook
12 | 10m | 20m

batter
2 cups cornflour
1 cup plain flour
¼ tsp baking powder
½ cup Greek-style, plain yoghurt, strained
3 tbsp rosewater
½ cup (125 ml) water

syrup
2 cups sugar
1¼ cup (310 ml) water
¼ cup (60 ml) rosewater
2 tbsp liquid saffron*
1 tsp citric acid
¼ tsp cardamom

for cooking
1 cup canola oil

1   In a mixing bowl, sift the cornflour together with plain flour and baking powder. Add the yoghurt, rosewater and water. Whisk together, until the mixture is smooth and lump-free. Set aside to settle for 30 minutes and then transfer the batter to a clean squeezy bottle.

2   Meanwhile, make the syrup. In a small saucepan, mix the sugar and water together and bring to the boil. Lower the heat to minimum and gently stir for 5 minutes, or until the sugar dissolves and the syrup thickens. Add the rosewater, liquid saffron, citric acid and cardamom and stir through. Continue to simmer, over the lowest heat setting, to keep warm.

3   In a medium-sized frying pan, heat the oil over a medium to high heat. Once the oil is hot, use tongs to place a 10 cm egg-ring into the oil. Squeeze the batter from the bottle into the egg-ring. Squeeze in a circular motion to create a spiral shape. Fry for 1 minute before removing the egg-ring and turning the spiral over. Cook for another minute, remove from the pan and drain on absorbent paper. Place the egg-ring once more into the oil and repeat with the remaining batter.

4   Once all the spirals are cooked, carefully place a single zoolbia into the prepared hot syrup. Make sure it is completely immersed. Let stand for 30 seconds in the syrup before removing and transferring to a plate to drain. Repeat with the remaining spirals. Note: Do not put the zoolbia on top of each other, or they will stick together.

note
*See page 18 for instructions on how to make liquid saffron.

tasty tip

Make the syrup the day before and reheat as required. This will produce a more intensely flavoured zoolbia.

fresh is best

For this dish, always choose the juiciest, freshest dates from the fresh food section of the supermarket, as opposed to the prepackaged, dried variety.

[pronounced / rang-ee-nak]

ranginak

DATE & WALNUT SLICE

1   Dry-fry the walnuts over a medium heat for 5 minutes, frequently stirring. Remove from the heat and cool.

2   Make a small, lengthwise cut to each date and remove the stone. Place a few of the cooled walnut pieces inside each date and press to close. Transfer the stuffed dates to a square, 15 cm dish, lined with baking paper. Place them in a single layer, and don't pack them in too tightly.

3   In a large, non-stick pan, melt the butter and fry the flour over a medium heat for 15 minutes, constantly stirring. The mixture will gradually change to a loose, fluffy consistency and turn a pale, caramel colour. Once ready, pour the hot mixture over the dates. Quickly smooth the surface with a spatula or wooden spoon.

4   Combine the icing sugar, cinnamon and cardamom together and dust over the slice. Garnish with the ground pistachio and shredded coconut.

5   Place in the refrigerator to cool and harden for 1 hour. Lift from the container and cut into squares.

serving suggestion
Delicious served with rose petal, cinnamon or cardamom tea. Recipes can be found on page 234.

makes	prep	cook	chill
20	15m	15m	1h

1 cup walnuts, roughly chopped
   into three or four pieces
2 cups fresh dates
1 cup butter
1½ cups flour
2 tbsp icing sugar
½ tsp cinnamon
1 tsp cardamom

garnish
2 tbsp ground pistachio
1 tsp shredded coconut

noon-e gerdooee

WALNUT COOKIES

makes 16 · **prep** 10m · **cook** 15m · **chill** 2h

3 egg yolks
½ cup sugar
1 tsp vanilla essence
1 tsp baking powder
1 tsp cardamom
1 tbsp rosewater
1½ cups walnuts

garnish
16 halved walnuts

1 Beat the egg yolks and sugar together, until the mixture is thick and pale. Add the vanilla essence, baking powder, cardamom and rosewater and mix well.

2 Finely chop the walnuts and add to the mixture. Stir gently, until all ingredients are thoroughly combined. Place the mixture in the refrigerator for 2 hours, to chill and stiffen slightly.

3 Preheat oven the to 160 °C. Line two large baking trays with baking paper, and grease lightly.

4 Place heaped teaspoons of the mixture onto the prepared trays. Leave approximately 5 cm between each, to allow for spreading. Place a walnut half on top of each cookie and gently press down.

5 Bake for 15 minutes, or until cooked through. Allow the baked cookies to cool slightly on the trays, before removing from the baking paper. Place on a wire rack to cool and dry out completely.

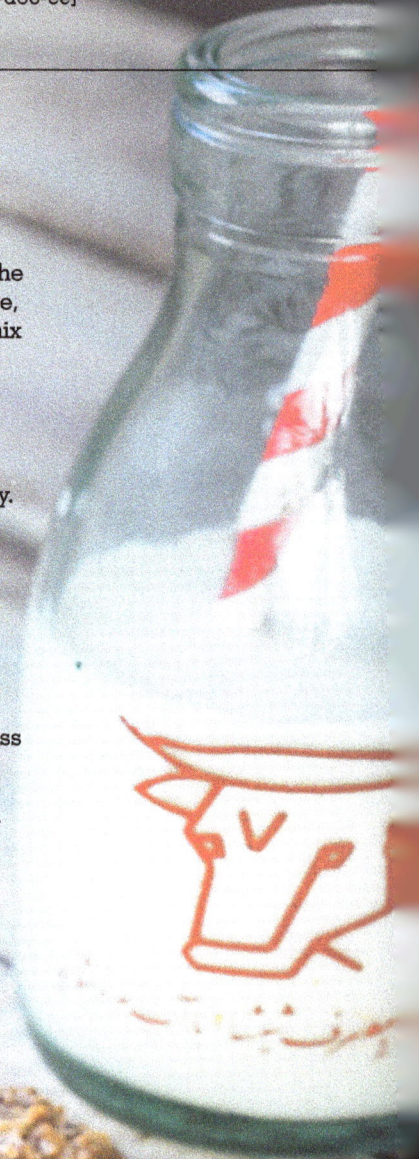

sohan

[pronounced / sew-haan]

SAFFRON BRITTLE

1 Wrap four 15 cm plates or trays in aluminium foil, grease lightly and
set aside.

2 In a large, non-stick pan, gently heat the wheatgerm, plain flour and
cardamom over a low heat for 1 minute, constantly stirring. Add the
caster sugar, brown sugar and rosewater and stir until the sugars
dissolve.

3 Add the butter, liquid glucose, honey and liquid saffron. Continue to
cook over a low heat, constantly stirring and folding the mixture for
45 minutes. The mixture will gradually change to a stiffer consistency,
turn a golden, caramel colour, and no longer stick to the pan.

4 Quickly spoon the mixture onto the prepared aluminium foil-lined
plates and flatten with the base of a glass. Garnish with the pistachio
slivers and rose petals, and once again using the base of a glass, lightly
press the pistachios and rose petals into the mixture.

5 Allow to cool to room temperature, before storing in a tin separated by
sheets of baking paper as the sohan sweats. These will keep for up to
2 weeks.

note
*See page 18 for instructions on how to make liquid saffron.

makes 4 10 cm sheets

prep 5m

cook 50m

½ cup wheatgerm
½ cup plain flour
1½ tsp cardamom
1 cup caster sugar
¼ cup brown sugar
½ cup rosewater
150g butter
1 tbsp liquid glucose
2 tbsp honey
2 tbsp liquid saffron*

garnish
3 tbsp slivered pistachio
dried rose petals (optional)

ackbar mashti

SAFFRON ICE CREAM

serves 8—10
prep 5m
freeze 1h

2 litres vanilla ice cream
½ cup thick double cream
2 tbsp liquid saffron*
3 tbsp rosewater
4 tbsp pistachios,
  roughly chopped

garnish
crushed pistachios

1   Place the ice cream in the refrigerator to soften slightly.

2   Meanwhile, line a tray with baking paper. Spread a thin layer of thickened cream, approximately ½ cm thick, over the baking paper. Place the tray in the freezer and freeze for 30 minutes, or until the cream is solid. Once frozen, roughly chop into 1 cm chunks and return to the freezer.

3   Once the ice cream has softened, transfer to a large bowl and mix with the liquid saffron and rosewater. Gently stir in the chopped pistachios and frozen cream chunks.

4   Return the ice cream to the freezer for 30 minutes, or until required.

serving suggestion
Serve in individual bowls or between wafers. Garnish with crushed pistachios.

note
*See page 18 for instructions on how to make liquid saffron.

[pronounced / gho-tob]

ghotab

ALMOND NUGGETS

1   In a medium-sized bowl, whisk the egg yolks, yoghurt and canola oil together.

2   Gradually add the sifted flour and baking powder. Continue whisking until all ingredients are thoroughly combined. Transfer the soft dough to a lightly floured chopping board and knead briefly. Wrap the dough in cling wrap and refrigerate for 1 hour.

3   Meanwhile, prepare the filling. In a small, non-stick pan, lightly toast the ground almonds and sugar over a low heat for 5 minutes, constantly stirring. Remove the pan from the heat, add the cardamom and rosewater and set aside to cool.

4   Divide the chilled dough into twenty even-sized pieces. Roll each piece into a small ball. Flatten each ball, with the palm of your hand and form a circle approximately ½ cm thick.

5   Place ½ teaspoon of the almond mixture onto the flattened dough. Fold over, to create a small ball or crescent shape and press the edges to seal.

6   Heat the oil, in a small, frying pan, and deep-fry the nuggets for 2–3 minutes, or until they turn a light, golden colour. Drain on absorbent paper and set aside to cool. Once cool, dust with the icing sugar and a sprinkling of crushed pistachio.

serving suggestion
Delicious served with rose petal, cinnamon or cardamom tea. Recipes on page 234.

makes	prep	chill	cook
20	30m	1h	10m

dough
2 eggs yolks
½ cup Greek-style, plain yoghurt
½ cup canola oil
1½ cups plain flour, sifted
1 tsp baking powder

filling
1 cup ground almonds
½ cup sugar
1 tbsp cardamom
2 tbsp rosewater

for cooking
½ cup canola oil

garnish
½ cup icing sugar
1 tbsp crushed pistachio

[pronounced / noon-eh nokh-od-chee]

noon-e nokhodchi

CHICKPEA FLOUR COOKIES

makes 80 | **prep** 30m | **cook** 30m

225 g butter
1 cup caster sugar
1 egg yolk
1 tsp ground cardamom
1 tbsp rosewater
2 cups roasted chickpea flour

garnish
4 tbsp slivered pistachios

1   Preheat the oven to 150 °C. Line a baking tray with greaseproof paper.

2   In a medium-sized bowl, beat the butter and caster sugar together until creamy. Add the egg yolk, cardamom and rosewater.

3   Gradually sift in the chickpea flour and fold through, until all ingredients are thoroughly combined.

4   Transfer the dough to a lightly floured chopping board and knead for 2 minutes. Roll the dough out to a thickness of 1½ cm. Use a 2 cm, four-leaf clover cookie cutter and gently press the cookies out of the dough. Transfer to the lined baking tray and decorate the top of each cookie with a single pistachio sliver.

5   Place the tray on the middle shelf of the oven and bake for 25 minutes. The baked cookies should be pale in colour and not overly browned. Remove from the oven, and allow to cool on the tray. Store in an airtight container.

serving suggestion
Delicious served with rose petal, cinnamon or cardamom tea. Recipes can be found on page 234.

handle with care

Caution: These cookies are extremely soft and crumble easily. So take care when handling.

noon berenji

RICE FLOUR COOKIES

1   Preheat the oven to 150 °C. Line a baking tray with greaseproof paper.

2   In a large bowl, whisk the butter and sugar together, until light and fluffy. Gradually add the rosewater and eggs. Continue to whisk, until thoroughly combined.

3   Sift the rice flour, baking powder and cardamom together. Gradually add to the mixture and fold through until all ingredients are combined.

4   Transfer the dough to a lightly floured chopping board and knead for 2 minutes. Roll the dough out to a thickness of ½ cm. Using a 3 cm cookie cutter, cut circles from the dough and transfer to the lined baking tray.

5   Using a toothpick or cookie cutter, press lightly on the top of cookie to make an imprint. Decorate with a sprinkle of poppy seeds.

6   Place the tray on the middle shelf of the oven, and bake for 15 minutes. The baked cookies should be pale in colour and not browned at all. Remove from the oven and allow to cool completely, on wire trays. Store in an airtight container for up to a week.

serving suggestion
Delicious served with rose petal, cinnamon or cardamom tea. Recipes can be found on page 234.

makes	prep	cook
24	15m	15m

250 g butter (softened)
1 cup sugar
2 eggs
¼ cup (60 ml) rosewater
3 cups rice flour
1 tsp baking powder
1 tsp cardamom

to decorate
2 tbsp poppy seeds

[pronounced / noon-eh nar-gill-ee]

noon-e nargili

COCONUT COOKIES

makes 16 | **prep** 10m | **cook** 20m

3 egg whites
¼ tsp cream of tartar
2 cups caster sugar
1 tsp vanilla extract
1 cup flour
3½ cups coconut flakes

garnish
½ cup coconut flakes
2 tbsp crushed pistachio

1   Preheat the oven to 150 °C. Line a baking tray with baking paper and grease lightly.

2   Whisk the egg whites and cream of tartar together, until soft peaks form.

3   Gradually add the sugar and vanilla extract. Continue whisking until the mixture turns glossy, and the peaks stiffen.

4   Add the flour gradually, fold through and beat until the mixture is smooth and even. Gently stir in the coconut flakes.

5   Take teaspoonfuls of the mixture and roll into balls. Roll the balls in the extra coconut flakes and place onto the lined baking tray. Flatten each ball slightly and garnish with a sprinkle of crushed pistachio.

6   Place the tray on the middle shelf of the oven and bake for 20 minutes. The baked cookies should be pale in colour, with slightly browned outer edges. Remove from the oven and let cool slightly on the trays before removing and placing on wire racks. Store in an airtight container for up to a week.

serving suggestion
Delicious served with rose petal, cinnamon or cardamom tea. Recipes can be found on page 234.

[pronounced / buk-laa-vaa]

baklava

SWEET FILO LAYERS WITH PISTACHIOS, ALMONDS & WALNUTS

1   Use a food processor to finely chop the almonds, pistachios and walnuts. Mix with the remaining filling ingredients. Set aside.

2   Preheat the oven to 180 °C. Grease a 30 cm x 20 cm, rectangular baking dish.

3   Place a sheet of filo pastry in the prepared baking dish, and brush lightly with a little of the melted butter. Repeat the same process with 19 more sheets. Note: Filo pastry dries out and cracks when it comes in contact with air. So, work quickly and cover the unused filo with a sheet of baking paper and a damp tea towel.

4   Spread the prepared filling evenly over the layers of filo.

5   Place a sheet of filo pastry on top of the filling, and lightly brush with a little of the melted butter. Repeat the process with the remaining 19 sheets. Use any torn sheets in the middle layers. Pour any remaining melted butter over the top of the baklava.

6   Use a sharp knife to cut small squares, approximately 4 cm in size. Cut through the top and bottom layers of the pastry.

7   Just before baking, lightly sprinkle the baklava with a little cold water. This helps prevent the pastry from curling. Bake for 45 minutes.

8   Meanwhile, make the syrup. In a small saucepan, gently heat the sugar, water, lemon juice, honey and cardamom over a low heat until the sugar dissolves. Increase the heat to medium and continue cooking for a further 5 minutes, or until the mixture thickens slightly. Remove from the heat and allow to cool.

9   Pour the cooled syrup over the hot baklava and allow to cool, unrefrigerated, for at least 4 hours. Garnish each baklava square with a sprinkling of crushed pistachio. Transfer to a sealed plastic container and refrigerate until needed.

note
If using frozen filo, defrost slowly in the refrigerator for 24 hours, prior to using.

makes 30 | prep 30m | cook 45m

40 sheets filo pastry
1 cup butter, melted

filling
2 cups blanched almonds
1 cup pistachios
1 cup walnuts
2 tbsp sugar
¼ tsp cinnamon
¼ tsp cardamom
2 tbsp rosewater
1 tbsp orange blossom water

syrup
2 cups sugar
1 cup (250 ml) water
1 tsp lemon juice
2 tbsp honey
½ tsp cardamom
2 tbsp rosewater
1 tbsp orange blossom water

garnish
1 tbsp crushed pistachio

[pronounced / faa-loo-deh]

faloodeh

ICY RICE NOODLES

1   In a small saucepan, bring the water to the boil. Add the sugar and stir over a medium heat until the sugar dissolves. Remove from the heat, add the rosewater and allow to cool to room temperature. Transfer the mixture to a suitable freezer container and freeze for 1 hour.

2   Meanwhile, place the noodles in a small saucepan. Add enough boiling water to cover completely and simmer for 10 minutes. Strain and rinse under cool water.

3   Remove the container from the freezer and rake the icy mixture with a fork. Add half of the noodles and stir through. Return to the freezer for another hour.

4   Again, rake the mixture with a fork, add the remaining noodles and stir though. Return to the freezer and continue to freeze for another 2 hours. Rake the mixture again, to break up any large, frozen clumps and return to the freezer until required.

serving suggestion
Remove from the freezer 15 minutes before serving. Once again rake, to fluff the mixture. Serve in individual bowls, garnished with a slice of lime, and a squeeze of lime juice.

variation: faloodeh makhloot
Faloodeh can also be served alongside Ackbar Mashti. See recipe on page 218.

serves
6

prep
5m

freeze
4h

1 cup (250 ml) water
1 cup sugar
¼ cup (60 ml) rosewater
125 g rice vermicelli noodles,
    cut into 3 cm lengths
garnish
¼ cup (60 ml) lime juice
lime slices

Good-quality, loose black tea is
naturally dark brown in colour
and consists of medium to large
leaves, with very little powder.

Persian tea is traditionally
brewed over a samovar.

[pronounced / chy-ee]

chai

CINNAMON, CARDAMOM & ROSE PETAL TEAS

serves
6

brew
10 -15m

water
loose, black tea leaves such as
   Darjeeling or Ceylon

additions
½ cinnamon stick
or 4 cardamom pods
or 1 tbsp dried rose petals

1   Fill the kettle with fresh water and bring it to the
boil.

2   Pour a little of the boiled water into your teapot to
warm. Swirl around the water then discard. Add
2 tablespoons of tea leaves to the teapot. Pour boiling
water over the tea leaves.

3   Place your teapot over a teapot warmer and brew
gently, for 10—15 minutes. At this stage, add your
choice of cinnamon stick, cardamom pods or rose
petals. Note: It is paramount that when brewing tea it
should never come to the boil. If tea is allowed to boil
it will turn bitter.

serving suggestion
To serve, pour a little of the brewed tea through a
strainer into each tea glass. Top with boiling water
and adjust the colour to your taste. Serve with cubed
or candied sugar. Persian tea should be rich and dark
in colour and is never served with milk.

index

thank you

Firstly, I would like to say thanks to Jamshid for all your help, insight and inspiration throughout this project. Also for always being available at a moment's notice for hand modelling, tray holding, and so on.

Secondly, a big thank you to Azar and Val for proofreading, editing and testing some of the recipes. Your feedback was invaluable.

Thank you to Vahid for proofreading and edits to the beginning sections and for always giving me a positive energy to finish the book.

Thank you to the lovely Jilla for modelling for the cover.

Thanks also to all our dear family and friends for all your encouragement and support over the years and thanks to all the wonderful Iranain cooks that inspired me.

www.ingramcontent.com/pod-product-compliance
Lightning Source LLC
Chambersburg PA
CBHW040318100426
42811CB00012B/1480